The Great Leveler

protect your innovations

SURENDRA VYAS

INDIA • SINGAPORE • MALAYSIA

Notion Press

No.8, 3rd Cross Street,
CIT Colony, Mylapore,
Chennai, Tamil Nadu – 600004

First Published by Notion Press 2020
Copyright © Surendra Vyas 2020
All Rights Reserved.

ISBN 978-1-63633-560-5

This book has been published with all efforts taken to make the material error-free after the consent of the author. However, the author and the publisher do not assume and hereby disclaim any liability to any party for any loss, damage, or disruption caused by errors or omissions, whether such errors or omissions result from negligence, accident, or any other cause.

While every effort has been made to avoid any mistake or omission, this publication is being sold on the condition and understanding that neither the author nor the publishers or printers would be liable in any manner to any person by reason of any mistake or omission in this publication or for any action taken or omitted to be taken or advice rendered or accepted on the basis of this work. For any defect in printing or binding the publishers will be liable only to replace the defective copy by another copy of this work then available.

Disclaimer

The opinions expressed in the book are those of the author and do not necessarily reflect the official policy or position of the author's current or past employers. The contents of the book should in no way be construed as legal advice and the reader should consult a professional for any consultation. Any resemblance or similarity to actual events is purely coincidental.

Dedication

Dedicated to all the COVID front line workers because of whom many like me could stay at home, do their regular work and even write a book.

Contents

Acknowledgement   9
Prologue   11

Chapter 0: A Negative Right   13
Chapter 1: The Scion Is Back   27
Chapter 2: The Cautious and the Daring   36
Chapter 3: Reinventing the Wheel   46
Chapter 4: The War Room   56
Chapter 5: Is Patent and Trademark the Same Thing?   66
Chapter 6: What the Patent   74
Chapter 7: Back to College   84
Chapter 8: Patent Family is Asexual   92
Chapter 9: Can She Do It?   104
Chapter 10: Having a Team Is Not the Same As Having a Strategy   115
Chapter 11: The Strategy and the Landscape   128
Chapter 12: IP, the Great Leveler   137

Thank You, Reader   145
Puzzle 1 (Easy) WordFind   147
Puzzle 2 (Difficult) The Great Leveler Crossword   149

Acknowledgement

Special thanks to Rohit Sukhija for the continuous nudge to inspire me to complete the book and for the chapter by chapter review.

Thanks to Pragathi MS, Sindhu Rao and Ankita Hore for the final draft review and constructive feedback.

Prologue

"Future Sensors? What is this company? Who is behind this? This sure is a conspiracy from some competitor of ours to slow us down. There has never been a patent infringement case in the domestic automobile tyre industry. We have always been cooperative with each other," fumed Mr. Chopra. He was infuriated more by the language used and the accusations made at his firm without any background or proof.

It was a plush boardroom with rich furnishings and state-of-the-art conferencing equipment. Behind Mr. Chopra was a showcase with a multitude of awards received by RoadKing over the years for business excellence and technical innovation in the tyre-manufacturing industry.

Swamy entered the room and could immediately sense the tension in the room and on everyone's faces. Roshni handed the letter over to him to read.

Roshni pulled Gowda's laptop and started browsing through the search results on Google for "Future Sensors". As she opened the home page of the company and started reading about the founders of the company, her face turned pale.

"It's a startup," Roshni almost whispered with a sense of despair concerning what she was about to say and then picked up her voice. "It's a startup," she repeated in a bolder voice, "a startup focusing on latest Artificial Intelligence based sensor technologies with a variety of applications in the automobile industry," she continued, faltering again, before ending her sentence, "and it is started and owned by Rocky Dandekar."

"Rocky Dandekar? Now, I understand." Mr. Chopra was bewildered. He seemed to have found some answers but was more infuriated than before.

Chapter 0

A Negative Right

"But why should we even have the concept of patents, isn't it stifling innovation?" asked one of the participants from the group.

Krish was conducting an Intellectual Property awareness session for the technology team members of one of his clients. While he loved his work overall as an IP entrepreneur, he loved most, the opportunity to interact with technology professionals and take them through the concept of innovation and Intellectual Property.

At the same time, it was not an easy task to engross a high-intellect, tech-aware and often coding-heavy group to the world of IP, which according to them was more about legalities and processes.

But Krish had his ways of engaging the audience. Laptops were a strict no during the session and non-participation was not an option. For him, the statement "let's keep the session interactive" was not just a formal sentence to say before starting the session.

He ensured he kept the session interactive through quizzes, activities, role-plays and various other tools to engage the participants.

So if one of the participants asked a question, it was a vindication for Krish that his engagement efforts were delivering results.

"Good question; let me explain with the help of a case study."

He had a mental bank of case studies for the regular questions and this was his favourite.

"Let's go back thousands of years in time, to the world of medieval kings and their decrees. Imagine a small village on the banks of a river making the soil fertile for farming throughout the year. The villagers paid obeisance to the king of the land. Almost everyone in the village was into farming, and one particular farmer amongst them was a smart and innovative but an eccentric farmer. He always came up with new ideas for solving problems related to farming. For example, for improving crop productivity, he would experiment with soil composition, use compost made out of waste, test hybrid seeds and many others. All these were great ideas that helped him get a better yield than other farmers, but he never shared his tricks with anyone else. Eccentric, he was."

Krish walked around the room as he spoke with an attempt to make eye contact with most of the participants. This was cited as a best practice in his training playbook to make the participants feel connected to the topic and the trainer. It also helped him sense the pulse of participation in the group.

Sensing a decent level of participation from the group, Krish continued with the case explanation.

"One of the major problems faced by farmers of the village was that of birds destroying crops. The farmers and their family members would take turns to keep an eye on the crops and ward off birds. But no one had a solution or even thought of coming up with one. You see, the first step towards innovation is accepting that you can solve the problem. There is always a solution. And who better to come up with a solution than our smart but eccentric farmer."

He went on, "After various experiments, he came up with what he called a strawman. He took two bamboo sticks, made a cross out of it, placed an earthen pot with face markings on top and fixed hay on the sticks. Sounds familiar? Yes, that was the first prototype of what the world would later come to know as a scarecrow. He secured it in his farm and it worked. It kept away the birds, as they perceived it as a living person.

While that solved a major problem, it also gave rise to a new problem. Unlike his previous ideas, this was out in the open. Other farmers could see it and built their own strawmen for their farms. Within a week, every farm in the village had a strawman. Our smart farmer was furious. He didn't want others to copy his idea, at least not without something in return. But he couldn't stop them.

Annoyed and frustrated, he went to the king with his complaint. The king heard him and turned to his most trusted economic adviser for a solution.

A discussion is now taking place between the farmer and the economic adviser of the king. Let's simulate that discussion. The left half of the group will represent the farmer and the right represents the economic adviser."

Krish turned to the left group.

"So farmers, let's start with you. What are your complaints?"

I created the strawman for myself; others do not have a right to use it without my permission.

I don't want them to use it, and if they do, they should give me something in return.

Just because it was in the open, it doesn't mean they can copy it.

I am smart and I know it, but I won't have any incentive to solve future problems if everyone blatantly copies it.

The participation level seemed to be high. Case studies with role-plays always yielded the highest interaction as per Krish's experience. He then moved to the group on the right.

"Now it's the economic advisers' group's turn, do you have any questions?"

How did you come up with this idea? Have you seen anything like this before?

You didn't create the pot for the first time or the bamboo sticks or the hay. All these items were known, you just combined them. How can you stop others from using your strawman if you are using things known in public knowledge?

Why did you put it out in the open if you didn't want others to copy it? You should have thought about it before doing that.

And how do you put a value to this idea? What do you want in return? A bag of rice or a box of eggs? Should it be a one-time exchange or a monthly-recurring transaction as long as they use the strawman?

"Greattt. That was a great discussion. After the discussion, the economic adviser turned back to the king and requested for a week's time to come up with a new decree to address the situation."

"Now let's all become the economic adviser and think of a solution. Any thoughts?" probed Krish.

I think the farmer should get some incentive for sharing his solution with others; else, as he said, he will not have any incentive to invent in the future or at least not share it with the public.

I agree, but there should be some cap on the incentive either in terms of benefits or in terms of time period beyond which it should be freely available for the public.

But how do we know, in the first place, if the farmer is the first one to really come up with the idea? There must be a registration and assessment process to confirm the inventorship and then provide those benefits to the farmer.

If the farmer is getting incentives, he should also have the obligation to share the details of the idea with the public and allow others to manufacture and sell on reasonable terms.

"Amazing. These are all excellent thoughts. The economic adviser took all considerations into account and created a new decree to protect the interests of creative farmers while keeping the societal benefits of innovation in mind. Our farmer was credited for his innovation under certain terms and conditions. And if you combine all this is in the form of modern law, this will be the patent system in a nutshell.

The whole idea of the patent system is to encourage inventors to solve problems and be rewarded for that in return for sharing their ideas with the public. In exchange for their ideas, they get a monopoly for a limited period to use, commercialize or licence their inventions. Beyond that period, the ideas become available for the public to use and build on.

It is a beautiful system and, if implemented effectively, it can significantly enhance the economic potential of society and country. Inventors are problem solvers. Industries are built and jobs are created based on new inventions. So, the patent system is aimed at enhancing innovation rather than stifling it, but like in all legal systems, it may be misused at times."

There was a sense of philosophical realism in Krish's tone as he looked at the original member who had asked the question.

"I have a question," said the head of the group sitting at the back, "what if another farmer builds a better version of the strawman by, say, adding wheels to it to make it move around the farm. Who gets the credit for that new strawman?"

"That's a great question and takes us to another interesting aspect of Intellectual Property but let's take that after the lunch break."

As the group stood for the break, some participants walked up to Krish for some follow-up queries and discussions. And as they were settling down at the lunch table, Krish pulled out his phone and switched it on. There were a number of missed calls and messages.

As he was going through some of the messages, the screen flashed up with a call from the number saved as "Roshni Tanya's Friend".

Hi Krish, this is Roshni, Tanya's friend. Hope you remember me.

Hey, sure I do. Hi Roshni. How are you?

I am good. Thanks. Do you have time for a quick chat?

Yeah. I am actually in the middle of lunch, which is in the middle of a training session. So, if it's real quick, sure.

Yeah, it'll be quick. I am in my office with our leadership team. There is an urgent issue that has come up and it relates to IP. I was wondering if we could meet and get your guidance on how to address it. Can you come over today?

Okay. I think I know the RoadKing office and actually, I'm not far from it. I can be there by 5:00 PM. Would that work?

Sure, see you then.

Krish switched off the phone again and finished his lunch.

The group reconvened after the break. Keeping a group engaged in a training session after lunch is an uphill task. But, again, Krish had his ways and, sometimes, it worked.

He made everyone stand. Everyone was encouraged to ask a question related to the topics covered before the break or answer any of the questions asked. As someone asked a question or answered one, he or she was allowed to sit. After some rounds of interesting questions and answers, everyone was sitting and reenergized.

It was his way of adding some fun and reclaiming the mind space of the participants for the rest of the session.

"Let's now take the question that the lady at the back asked before the break. Ma'am, can you please repeat the question?"

"So, about the strawman, what if another farmer builds a better version of the strawman by, say, adding wheels to it to make it move around the farm. Who gets the credit for that new strawman?"

"That's an interesting question and brings us to a very unique aspect of Intellectual Property rights."

"First of all, let us understand this. Like many other legal and fundamental rights, IP rights are rights given to you by the legislature under specific terms and conditions. Similar to the right to freedom, right to speech and other such rights. But the unique part of IP right, unlike any other right, is that it is a negative right. Now, what do you mean by a negative right? An IP right is a negative right because it gives you a right to stop others from using or commercializing your invention without your permission or a licence. So you can stop others, but you yourself may or may not use it, hence negative.

The concept of a negative right is sometimes difficult to explain but the question the lady asked brings out the meaning very effectively. So, thanks for asking the question, ma'am.

Taking the example of the strawman, let us first assume that our first farmer gets a patent for his idea of a strawman. This gives him the right to stop others from using or selling the strawman without his permission. Now, he is not the only smart guy in the world.

Say, another farmerette, which is female for a farmer, in the village takes the idea and modifies it to add wheels so that the strawman can easily move around a large farm and be placed wherever required. Now, can she get a patent for this idea and can she stop the original inventor farmer or others from using it?"

There was silence as Krish waited for any answer or thoughts from the participants. In situations like these, Krish would force volunteer an answer. He walked to the centre-right side of the room and sat down next to a guy.

"What do you think?" he asked.

"I don't know." The guy was taken unaware.

"You don't know, but you may have some thoughts. What should happen in such a scenario?"

"As you said, patent is a negative right, so I think she should not get a patent as she has copied the original idea from the farmer" was the response.

Krish stood up and walked back to the front. Getting the first response from a group is important to get others to speak even if it is completely wrong as in this case. Beyond the first response, the group generally becomes active and multiple responses start coming.

And so it happened in this case. Multiple members started sharing their thoughts. Most of them suggested against granting a patent to the farmerette although the reasoning varied.

"Hmm. Interesting. However, patent law does not think so. The farmerette is eligible for a patent on the improvement of the known strawman, assuming it is a new idea and not done before. However, the interesting part is about the rights that come with that patent for the farmerette."

"The question is, can she commercialize it? As in, can she build such wheeled strawmen and sell it in the market? That's where the concept of negative right comes in."

"The idea of a wheeled strawman builds upon the idea of a regular strawman. Our original farmer owns the patent for a regular strawman, and the farmerette owns the patent for the wheeled strawman. Hence, both can stop each other from commercializing their inventions. In this case, the farmerette can stop the farmer from selling the wheeled strawman, but she also can't sell it unless she has a licence from the farmer for the regular strawman. And that is the essence of a negative right."

"Sounds complicated? It is, a bit. Just run it through your mind once again, and let me know if you have any questions."

The session continued until around 4:45 PM, after which Krish left the building and booked an Uber to the RoadKing office. The app showed 12 minutes to the destination.

Nine Months Back

Chapter 1

The Scion Is Back

The Kempegowda International Airport at Bangalore is one of the busiest airports in the country. Thanks to the booming software industry in the city, the airport facilitates the frenetic movement of domestic and international travel in and out of the city. The new swanky airport was inaugurated in 2008, facing much resistance from frequent travellers due to the location of the airport, which was miles away from the older airport in the heart of the city.

The infamous Bangalore traffic required air travellers to add in an extra couple of hours to ensure they reached in time for their flights. However, over the last decade, the airport has established itself as a world-class international airport with a multitude of amenities for travellers and visitors and multiple modes of transport to reach the airport. The metro rail works in progress would be the final step towards seamlessly integrating the airport with the rest of the city.

It was 2 AM on a Saturday. Mr. Chopra was dropped by his chauffer, Manju, outside the arrivals terminal of the airport. While Manju drove the Audi towards the premium parking area, right across the terminal, Mr. Chopra headed towards his favourite filter coffee stall. The arrivals terminal was abuzz with white-clothed pickup drivers holding placards with names of their pickups; some jaded and some elated travellers walking out of the arrivals gate and those who had come to welcome their family and friends arriving from different parts of the world. Mr. Chopra was one of those. He was there to welcome his only daughter Roshni who was returning from the US after completing her Masters in Rubber Technology and MBA from the University of Illinois at Urbana Champagne or UIUC, as it is commonly known.

Sipping his strong South Indian filter coffee without sugar, Mr. Chopra checked the flight status on his phone. The status refreshed itself to "Just landed", which meant it would be at least another 30 minutes before Roshni cleared the immigration, security, baggage and customs and exited the airport.

The arrival and departure terminals at places of travel, be it an airport, a train station or a bus stand, often rekindles old memories and emotions. A childhood train journey, a flight in the time of a family emergency or a fun-filled bus ride with friends, all come to mind. Gulping the last sip of his coffee, Mr. Chopra was reminded of the train journey with his family from their hometown of Ludhiana in the early 60s to the small peaceful town of Bangalore. His father had accepted the job of a finance head at a medium-sized tyre-manufacturing firm in a rather unconventional move in those times. It was a huge cultural change for his family to move from lively and boisterous Punjab to a soft, laidback Bangalore. The food, the language, the people, the climate, everything was as far apart as it could be. However, the family adapted and adapted positively. It is a result of that adaptation that today, Mr. Chopra could speak fluent Kannada and loved his filter coffee. The climate obviously was a change for the better and people were very accommodating. Bangalore had been their home for three generations now.

His string of thoughts was broken by the sound and visuals of Roshni waving, shouting and rushing out of the exit gate. Dressed in comfortable palazzo pants and a long cardigan, Roshni looked fresher than any of the other travellers even after 23 hours of the journey, including 20 hours inside the flight.

"She has gone through tough times and learnt a lot about the world ever since she left home for college," Mr. Chopra mumbled to himself and moved towards Roshni. Both looked in each other's eyes for a moment and hugged.

"Okay, let me guess," started Roshni with a huge smile. "Manju is in the parking, waiting for your missed call. You had your favourite filter coffee and you were reminiscing of the days when Grandpa moved from Ludhiana to Bangalore. Right?"

"Almost there." Mr. Chopra smiled back. "I was also thinking about you and your days ahead, it's going be challenging and exciting. I hope you are prepared."

"I am. But for now, let's get back home quick. I need to get over with the jetlag this weekend."

A few minutes later, Manju arrived at the pickup point; both alighted in the Audi as it raced out of the airport onto the road leading to the city. The road for a few kilometres outside the airport was unlike that of the rest of the city, it was wide, well marked, without any potholes and with a beautiful display of flowers on the divider stretch and murals depicting local culture on the sides of the road.

It was almost 4 AM as the car took an exit from the highway and entered the smaller road when Manju slowed down to manoeuvre the barricades set up by the traffic police to slow down the airport cab drivers and freewheeling bike riders. The cops stopped the car and checked Manju with a breathalyzer for alcohol consumption before they let them go.

"So, now that you are back after a whole 5 years, does it feel good to be back home?" asked Mr. Chopra.

"Know what, Dad? I never felt I was away, thanks to WhatsApp video calls; we anyways talked every Sunday, I was in touch with all my friends here and know all that's happening in their lives. Some of them are hitched, some married and some busy with their day jobs."

"That compels me to ask, as a father, any updates on your relationship status?"

"Hmmm... things are happening, but this is not the right time; when the time is right, you will be the first one to know, till then, no questions."

"Ok, ok, I am waiting!"

Manju was an excellent driver who had served the Chopra family for over two decades. He not only knew the routes and driving etiquettes, but he also very well knew the emotions of the Chopras. As the car drove past the Palace Ground Road, he purposely slowed down a bit to let Mr. Chopra peek out to get a view of a dilapidated office building on the left of the road. That was the building where Mr. Chopra Senior first opened a small office after he left his job with the firm he was employed with. No words were exchanged as both Roshni and her father looked at each other, realizing the importance of the moment. Whatever they were today, it was because of the entrepreneurial spirit of Mr. Chopra Senior who endured hardships and hard work to build a business empire from scratch.

The car picked up speed again and moved ahead a few kilometres before turning left in a direction away from the Chopra House in the posh Sadashivnagar locality.

"Whoa, are you planning to kidnap me, Manju?" asked Roshni. "I have been away, but I have lived long enough in Bangalore to know that this road does not lead to Sadashivnagar." Manju stayed on course without uttering a word, knowing well that the answer would come from his master.

"We are going to Whitefield," answered Mr. Chopra, "to your new apartment."

"Whitefield? My apartment? What's happening?" questioned a puzzled Roshni.

Mr. Chopra's voice transformed into a serious fatherly tone as he spoke. "Roshni, as I explained to you in our last call, the time has come. The time has come for you to prepare yourself to take over the reins of the company. And it doesn't happen in a day. And I don't want to impose it on you the way it happened for me. I want you to learn it and earn it. You sure would have a head start, but you will have to learn fast and work your way up. This is the first step of the challenge I have for you. We have an apartment in a residential complex in Whitefield, not far away from our manufacturing facility. Many of our staff members live there. I have got the apartment prepared for you to rent." Mr. Chopra emphasized on the word "rent".

"Starting Monday, you will join RoadKing Tyres as Chief of Staff to the CEO, that is me. Your role would involve managing business priorities and helping the CEO in critical projects and decision-making. This is a 24/7 job, and I expect you to be always updated with business insights and be available with the right information. While you are educationally qualified, you still do not have any relevant experience except for a couple of internships. I am taking a leap here by offering you this position, and I hope you won't disappoint. You will be on one-year probation after which we will decide the next course of action based on your performance."

"Hold on, hold on; I have just landed after a 24-hour journey, I'm exhausted, the jet lag is about to kick in; I was hoping to take a break, meet my friends, go for a vacation... I knew you had plans for me, but can't that wait like for a month for me to refresh and then start?" Roshni sort of revolted, knowing well that the chances of her being heard were zilch.

Roshni and anyone else who had known Mr. Chopra for long or had worked with him knew well that it was impossible to change his mind once he had taken a decision. The only person with such superpower was her mother who, unfortunately, succumbed to cancer the year Roshni left for the US. To Mr. Chopra's favour, his decisions had given a good return and he had rarely gone wrong with them.

"Vacations can wait. The islands and beaches of South East Asia are not going to be submerged underwater any time soon even by the worst doomsday predictions of the climate change supporters. And you need money to go on vacations. You will get a decent salary, which will help you pay the rent and afford a refined lifestyle. But you will still have to save for a few months, maybe a year before you can afford a vacation."

He went on, "Roshni, you are young, you are smart, you are ambitious; you have the Ivy League education and you have the entrepreneurial Chopra blood. But you sorely lack experience on the ground. Business cannot be managed from boardrooms unless you know the pulse of the staff and stakeholders. That is the experience I want you to get in the next one year so that you are ready for the next phase of the business world."

There was silence in the car for the rest of the journey as the car moved towards Whitefield and reached the entrance security clearance at the Star Homes Apartments in the Whitefield suburbs of Bangalore. It was just around five in the morning and early joggers were out on the streets. The air was still fresh and a few hours away from being contaminated by the insane traffic of private vehicles, buses, cabs and two-wheelers.

Star Homes was one of the many such apartments in Whitefield catering to the thousands of IT professionals living in the area and employed by the Who's Who of the IT world. The way apartment complex ran was a microcosm of the concept of Indian diversity—Indians from different regions of the country, speaking different languages, with diverse eating habits, following different religions, different educational backgrounds, all living together, sharing common amenities, working towards keeping the complex clean—much like the whole country was running.

Manju parked the car in the basement of Tower 1 and Mr. Chopra escorted Roshni to the 5th floor of the tower into a cozy two-bedroom unit. The flat was done to taste with wooden flooring, layered curtains, chic modular furniture and contemporary art décor.

"I hope you like it."

"Not that I have a choice, but it does look great," Roshni smiled back in a way accepting the diktat of her father on the upcoming challenge.

"Take rest now. See you in office, Monday morning."

Roshni took a long shower after her father left and treated herself to a soothing cup of sleep-inducing chamomile tea as the jet lag started to take over her body clock.

Soon, she was lying on the bed staring at the wall art Buddha painting in a Zen meditation stance. "I am going to need a lot of that in the days ahead."

Chapter 2

The Cautious and the Daring

"Good morning, sir," Roshni greeted her father and boss as he entered his office.

"What's the morning brief?"

"We'll start the day with the regular business news and updates. I have the daily bulletin ready. We will then visit the Chambers of Commerce to submit your nomination for the chairman of the Tyre-Manufacturing Association. Our team is in touch with all other members to ensure that you have an unchallenged victory for the post. You then have a lunch meeting planned with the State Industries Minister where, among other topics, you will be presenting a proposal for a reduction in customs duty for the import of rubber. In the afternoon, you are invited to inaugurate the childcare facilities at our factory premises for our employees to bring in their children during summer vacations."

The childcare facility was Roshni's idea immediately after she met with some of the women employees in her first week to understand their problems. Roshni realized there was not a single woman in the top brass of the RoadKing leadership and, hence, the decisions made did not adequately reflect diversity concerns.

Beyond diversity, there were other topics of business and people strategy at RoadKing that conflicted with Roshni's global perspective, developed through her internships and exposure. However, she realized that she would first have to establish herself before she could bring in foundational changes. It would be a long road ahead but one she was willing to take. The childcare facility was a small step in that direction.

It had been over two months since Roshni had taken the role of the chief of staff. She was going through the initial rigmarole of adjusting in a new setup and culture. The role was arduous and the boss was demanding. Her father expected her to know everything about everything. This required her to spend late nights every night preparing for the meetings and engagements for the next day. She was learning more every day than she learnt every month during her MBA. She was reading through technology briefs, annual reports, cash flow statements, business news, global market updates and employee benefit programmes. Every morning, she would prepare a daily bulletin of the business news and updates relevant to the industry from across the world.

"You also have a dinner meeting with Mr. Gowda and Mr. Swamy at home and the agenda of the meeting says 'Confidential'." Roshni continued with the briefing to her father.

"Yes. That is important. And I want you to be at that meeting. We are working with Forest Automobile of Germany on a highly confidential and high-value project code-named Project VC. For now, it's only Gowda, Swamy and me at RoadKing who are aware of the details of Project VC. I want you to spend a few hours with Gowda and Swamy today so that they can bring you up to speed on the project. You will lead this project and this is a part of your challenge. Rather, this is the real challenge."

In the last two months, ever since Roshni started shadowing her father on business meetings and strategic discussions, she always knew there would be a moment when she would be pushed into something big. This seemed to be the moment. This was the real challenge. Not that she was prepared, but again, she didn't have an option.

Mr. Vishwanath Gowda was a longtime confidant of Mr. Chopra and had been heading the Legal and Finance department at RoadKing for over 20 years now. Prior to that, he used to work at a law firm employed by RoadKing to manage its legal matters. However, as the company grew and the legal matters grew with it, Mr. Chopra poached Gowda to set up an in-house legal and finance department for RoadKing. Mr. Gowda now had an important role, which involved managing all sorts of issues ranging from reviewing vendor agreements to liaising with government officials and handling real estate discussions and, last and often the least, some employee matters. Needless to say, he was THE most important person in the company besides Mr. Chopra himself.

Mr. Swaminathan Natarajan, on the other hand, was a relatively recent addition to the RoadKing family. With a Bachelor's degree in Chemical Engineering from Anna University, Chennai and a Masters from IIT Madras, Swamy was a veteran in the automobile industry, having worked at the research division of a leading automobile manufacturer at Chennai for over 20 years. He took the plunge to join RoadKing to lead their technology efforts six years back. RoadKing did not have much of a technology division before Swamy joined. The focus had been more on manufacturing efficiencies and supply chain management and still was. According to Mr. Chopra, technology was good to have and did give intermittent benefits but could never be the thrust of the manufacturing business. *At least that was what he believed until some time back.*

Mr. Chopra, like his other top men, recruited Swamy after having known him for some time. He had regularly met Swamy at industry conferences and seminars and was hugely impressed by his technical prowess and vision for the industry. After a lot of thought, finally, Mr. Chopra succumbed to his own uncertainty and decided to take a chance with technology. He offered Swamy the opportunity to join RoadKing and move to Bangalore, which he knew Swamy had been yearning for, for long. Money was not a motivation for Swamy, but he insisted on full autonomy regarding technology-related decisions and full freedom to explore and experiment with new ideas and research. Mr. Chopra was not used to such negotiations but agreed with some hesitation and caveats.

Swamy had since grown a small team of five technologists and implemented various efficiency improvement technologies in the manufacturing plant. Some of those resulted in significant cost savings while some others were yet to be proved. Overall, nothing path-breaking from a technology perspective that could shift the focus from the company's reliance on supply chain and manufacturing to technology.

That was until Swamy came to Mr. Chopra six months back with the results of the research that he and his team were working on for more than two years. Sticking to the autonomy agreement, Mr. Chopra never questioned Swamy and his team unless they came back to him for some requirements, budget approvals or results. So, he had no clue what was about to come.

Mr. Chopra, although not a technology aficionado, would always keep himself abreast of the latest happenings in the automobile industry in terms of technology trends just so he did not miss out on something revolutionary. He was very well aware of the Kodak moment concept. What Swamy presented to him that day was truly revolutionary and never seen before in the tyre-manufacturing industry. There were rumours of various teams experimenting on such concepts globally, but none seemed to be at this advanced stage with this level of efficiency.

It seemed like his investment in technology was finally yielding. Another example of the high return on his decision-making.

Mr. Chopra immediately summoned Gowda to discuss strategy around developing the concept presented by Swamy. Gowda, being the astute legal and financial mind that he was, suggested vetting the technology and collaborating with someone having an equal stake in the game as a first step. He was even lesser sold on technology than Mr. Chopra was. He had seen many such innovations come and go and end up converting billionaires to millionaires.

"We have a Video Call with Mr. van Guard of Forest tomorrow 3 PM IST. The meeting tonight is to discuss the strategy for this project and our partnership with Forest Auto. This is the biggest bet our company has taken on technology, and the successful implementation of this project will thrust RoadKing onto the global automobile map."

After going through the morning bulletin, Roshni immediately instructed Sumitha, Mr. Chopra's admin, to convene a meeting of hers with Mr. Gowda and Mr. Swami in the Hampi meeting room. The Karnataka culture was so ingrained in the Chopra family that the Chopra Senior named all meeting rooms after famous tourist destinations in Karnataka. Apart from Hampi, there was a Mysore, Coorg, Gokarna, Udupi, Mengaluru and Badami.

"Good Morning, Roshni Ma'am," greeted Mr. Gowda as the three of them settled in the Hampi meeting room with a spectacular painting depicting the ruins of the Vijaynagara empire of Hampi adorning the walls.

"How many times have I told you, Mr. Gowda, to call me by my first name? You are way senior to me. And you too, Mr. Swami. Please don't call me ma'am ever again. Dad asked me to connect with both of you to know all there is to know about some highly confidential 'Project VC'. He wants me to take a lead on this, and I have no clue what VC even stands for. So, let's get started ASAP. I will also need my time to self-debrief and prepare for the dinner meeting."

"Roshni ma... sorry," Mr. Gowda fumbled and picked up again. "Roshni, before we get into the details, you need to appreciate the context of this project. If this goes ahead, this will be the biggest investment we will have ever made into any project, that too, a technology backed project. We have invested in new plants, new machinery, on entering new markets in the past, but this is unchartered territory for us."

"And also if this succeeds, which I am sure it will, this will be something the world of technology has never seen before," interrupted Swamy with an optimistic tone of a researcher.

"Roshni, I would like to believe that you have more faith in technology than your father and Mr. Gowda here have. Having studied and worked in the west, you have seen how technology has transformed the lives and industries there. We have adopted a lot of that technology in our daily life here in India, but the adoption in industry and, more specifically, the manufacturing industry is sluggish. We are ready to adopt anything that is proven and can give us immediate cost-benefit on a small investment but we are not ready to commit big investments to develop the technologies of the future," continued Swamy.

He went on. "When I joined RoadKing, I joined on the premise of research. I took that promise from Mr. Chopra. I told him that I could easily bring in cost savings through technological changes in the manufacturing and supply chain that would warrant my and my team's salary, but I wanted him to give me enough leverage to experiment on new ideas that would be revolutionary for the world, to say the least. I hired the best technology professionals, I repeat, technology professionals, not just engineers—technology professionals who had the passion to build products through pure science and research. We have, together, worked on multiple projects in the last six years, ranging from the manufacturing of tyres using recycled plastic to modular tyres that can automatically be readjusted for different vehicle sizes. But all this time, there was one dream project that my team was working on, which finally showed enough consistent results for us to be confident to take it beyond our labs to a pilot level. That's when I took it to Mr. Chopra."

He concluded, "Roshni, what I am going to explain to you is the essence of our technology but in very simple non-technical terms. This will be somewhere between a pitch to an investor and a detailed presentation to a technology leader. Your father has already made the investment decision. You now have to lead this project as a business manager. To be honest, and at the edge of being blasphemous, I am more confident about you leading this on the business front than your father."

Mr. Gowda and Mr. Swami exchanged foul looks. The relationship between the two was interesting as both were totally committed to the interest of the company and the family, but both had different styles of exhibiting the same. While Gowda was the loyal confidant to Mr. Chopra, Swamy embodied the risk-taking intrepreneur. While Gowda believed in the conservative style of business and finance, Swamy was always ready to challenge the status quo. At the same time, both had immense respect for each other. Roshni could see the dichotomy of the relationship and the need to balance the two if she had to lead this project.

"Before he gets into the details of his technology, I want you to take a realistic view," cautioned Mr. Gowda. "It is easy to get swayed away by the dreams of technology nirvana and global business control if the technology succeeds. While I totally support the idea and see the potential, my job is to be cautious, always. The idea looks great, the technology sounds fabulous and the business potential is unprecedented. But this won't be the first revolutionary idea in the technology and business world. The rate of success of big launches by industries across the world has never been great. Be it the New Coke in 1985, Orkut by Google or Amazon's Fire Phone. You can even google for Ford Edsel and Sony Betamax. Products may not work for a variety of reasons beyond the control of the owners and inventors. Hence, it is always better to take a phased approach and hedge your risks rather than investing big upfront."

"Ok. I have had enough of context. Now can I hear the billion-dollar idea that has the potential to change the automobile industry?" quipped an amused Roshni.

Chapter 3

Reinventing the Wheel

"I will let Swamy talk about it. It is his brainchild," said Gowda munching on his *thepla*.

Lunch was served for the three in the Hampi meeting room. Swamy had his homemade *pongal* and buttermilk. Roshni had ordered a paneer tikka sandwich and a latte from the CCD outside the office. And Gowda had an odd Gujarati lunch plate with *thepla*, *undhiyu* and *aamras*.

Gowda, although hailing from a traditional Kannadiga family of Bangalore, had developed a distaste for regular South Indian cuisine. During his tenure with the previous law firm, he was posted in Surat, Gujarat, for four years and that's when he fell in love with Gujarati cuisine. While returning to Bangalore from Surat, he convinced his local cook there to come along with his family to Bangalore. He had never since looked back upon idly or dosa.

"The name 'Project VC' was your idea. So, why don't you take the lead explaining that? I will take it further. By the way, Roshni, would you like to take a guess at what the C in VC stands for?" said Swamy savouring his buttermilk.

"Hmmm... Chopra," fathomed Roshni impulsively taking another sip of her latte.

"That's a bit self-indulging. I would have expected your father to have made a guess like this," Swamy replied nonchalantly. "Over to you, Gowda."

Roshni was left a bit embarrassed. She was not the one to impose family ownership in any professional context. However, the fact that she guessed "Chopra for C" implied otherwise. She was reminded of the lecture by Prof. Wallace in her Organizational Behaviour class at UIUC and made a mental note to work on her subconscious bias.

Gowda stood up with crumbs of thepla falling from his shirt and moved towards the whiteboard. He drew a circle on the board and added some spokes to it. Without risking another guess from Roshni, he started speaking.

"The C stands for Chakra. The word Chakra, as you know, has its origins in Sanskrit and has many different meanings. In philosophical and biophysical terms, it means a centre of *shakti* or energy in the human body or the universe. In a literal sense, it means a circle or a wheel representing movement. In mystical realms, it denotes specific shapes or diagrams for summoning spirits. From Sudharshan Chakra to Ashok Chakra to

Tantric Chakras, Chakra has always been an important concept in the Indian culture, religion, politics and business. For our project, Chakra embodies both a circle and a source of energy. That was the 'C'. Swamy, you can talk about the "V" in VC."

Gowda paused and gestured for Swamy to take over.

"Roshni, you must have heard of the peak oil theory. According to various leading technology and business research houses, we have already crossed the peak oil point. In simple terms, it is the point in time after which global production of oil and gas would begin to decline. The future for automobiles is going to be non-oil and non-gas. Major oil & gas companies across the world are transforming their businesses to adapt to a renewables-focused energy world.

The V in VC stands for Vidyut, which means 'electricity' in Sanskrit. Therefore, VC is Vidyut Chakra or Electric Wheel. In the automobile world, the future is electric vehicles. It won't be an exaggeration if I say that in a decade, we will completely move from liquid-fuel-powered vehicles to electric vehicles.

But there are still many technological, business, infrastructural and regulatory hurdles to overcome before we arrive at the omnielectric future. The biggest challenge in the growth of electric vehicles, as we all know, is Range Anxiety. The fear of having your car battery discharged before you reach your destination.

Every year, we are making progress in battery storage capacity and efficiency. But the thought of charging your vehicle more often than filling up petrol or diesel is a mental block that still stops many from switching. The need for additional infrastructure for charging does not help either. The electric vehicle may be a cute little second car to have but is far from confidently being the primary vehicle for a family at an affordable cost.

The automobile majors, battery research groups and even the software giants are all working on solutions for Range Anxiety, and they are delivering better performance every year. But no one expects a tyre-manufacturing firm like us to solve this problem because we don't have any skin in the game. We never had any incentive to innovate. Be it electric vehicle or combustion engine vehicle, cars will always need tyres. So, Range Anxiety is not our problem to solve.

But our team looked at it from a different angle. If you think of it, the car tyre has been the most modest yet the most important part of the vehicle since the inception of cars. The interiors of cars have become jazzy, the accessories have become trendier, the colours have gone metallic, but the tyre has remained humble. We have done away with gears, we have substituted the combustion engine, we are even planning to eliminate the driver, but the tyre is here to stay. You can't imagine a car without a tyre. So, we strongly believed that the solution to Range Anxiety can come from a tyre. The tyre of a future electric vehicle need not be the same as the tyre of current vehicles.

This is where we started brainstorming. In my years of research and innovation, one mantra I always followed was the 'Can we' principle. 'Can we' helps you to imagine.

'Can we fly like birds?' the Wright brothers would have thought.

'Can we send a message across the world by the click of a button?' Tim Berners Lee would have wondered.

'Can we further divide atoms into smaller particles?' Marie Curie would have frustratingly deliberated till she discovered radioactivity.

'Can we...'"

"Can we please take a bio break?" interrupted Gowda and walked towards the washroom.

There was silence in the room as both waited for Gowda to return.

By now, Roshni was totally captivated by the context provided by Swamy. She had some clue where this might be going but perhaps didn't have the imaginative heroism to even think if that was technologically possible.

That was exactly the mental space Swamy wanted Roshni to be in before he hit her with the final narrative. Swamy was experiencing what could be called intellectual orgasm for a researcher. He knew the look on the face of his audience as they were mesmerized by the creative possibilities of his ideas. He could see that look on Roshni's face. He was loving it.

"So the question that we asked ourselves was," Swamy continued as Gowda settled back in his chair, *"can we modify the humble tyre to solve the problem of energy storage in an electric vehicle?* And we believed we could. Our target was to build a tyre that could house a battery with higher energy storage capacity than regular batteries. This required two solutions. First, a modification in the material used for tyre manufacturing, and second, an improvement in the energy storage capacities.

Our quest for energy storage improvement led us to explore a fascinating new field of science— nanotechnology, which simply explained is the study of nanoparticles and is an emerging area for researchers across the world. Nanoparticles are literally 'small particles' and lie at the cusp of bulk materials and atomic particles and, hence, can claim to have the best of both the worlds. The unique properties of nanoparticles make them useful in a variety of applications ranging from electronics to cosmetics. Nanotechnology is being used to make clothes that are stain resistant, sunscreen that can absorb carcinogenic UV rays, bandages that can better contain a wound.

The use of nanotechnology in energy storage is an ongoing research and is showing promise, but there are challenges. The major challenge faced by researchers is to maintain the electrolyte of the battery at a higher pressure to improve the energy storage capacity. The more nanoparticles used, the higher the pressure required, which makes it impractical for the size of a battery used in an electric vehicle. It requires a much larger surface area, which would increase the weight of the battery.

The batteries for electrical vehicles are compared based on energy density, which as per the basic definition of density is the amount of energy stored per unit mass of the battery. Li-ion batteries currently claim to have the highest energy densities in the range of 250-300 Wh/kg. At this rate, the weight of the battery required to provide enough charge for a 400-km range may exceed 500 kg of battery weight. Totally impractical!

Due to battery size limitations, not much research was done on the use of nanoparticles at higher pressure. This is where we saw an opportunity. We were able to leverage this challenge, as we were not creating a battery, we were creating a tyre.

Across larger surface areas and at much higher pressure, we were able to achieve a 50-fold increase in the energy storage capacity in our labs by injecting higher amounts of Lithium nanoparticles in the electrolyte of a regular Lithium-Ion solution.

The next challenge was to incorporate this into a tyre. And when I earlier said that we wanted the tyre to house the battery, I didn't mean physically house it, I meant house it chemically. The chemicals of the battery should be infused in the rubber of the tyre.

We knew the normal rubber used for tyre manufacturing would not be able to handle the pressure required. The idea was to create a tyre with multiple layers. The outer and inner layer will be a novel material that can act as a covering to allow chemical reactions that happen in a battery. Between these two layers will be three layers corresponding to the anode, cathode and the electrolyte of the battery. We needed a novel composition for this new tyre material and we didn't have to go far.

If you recall, the Formula One Grand Prix was held in India in 2013. At that time, we did some experiments for the racecar tyres. The synthetic rubber used for manufacturing racecar tyres is very different for that used in regular tyres. It can handle much higher pressures as is required due to the high speed in the racing.

Although I can say it in one sentence in a few seconds now, it took us months of research to polymerize a novel material with the base as the race car tyre synthetic rubber, which could form the inner and outer layer in the new tyre design."

Roshni, who had been listening with astonishment till now finally spoke, "So, you have built a tyre which could chemically house a battery. So, the tyre is the battery?"

"Yes! the tyre is the battery and the battery is the tyre," Swamy's excitement was at its peak. "But we didn't stop there. We took it one step further. We now wanted to make the tyre self-sufficient and independent of additional charging infrastructure requirement. Remember, Range Anxiety is what we started with as the challenge. You may have heard of the regenerative brake technology, which stores and utilizes the kinetic energy of the vehicle generated during braking. We were able to modify the technology to store much higher amounts of energy by combining energy generated during braking as well as friction between the tyres and the ground. And since the storage is distributed across the four tyres of the car, we can store much higher amounts of energy than regular regenerative braking. Essentially, you will never have to recharge the tyre, I mean, battery of the vehicle as long as you keep using it."

Swamy paused wanting to hear the final reaction from Roshni who still seemed to be digesting the seemingly sci-fi description she had just heard.

At this point, Gowda shared his thoughts, giving some more time for Roshni to react.

"We have not only eliminated the need for a battery in an electrical vehicle, but we have also eliminated the need for charging. This invention will have significant ramifications on the future of electric vehicles. Not only on the energy storage front but also on the design and efficiency of vehicles. If you have seen inside the hood of an electric vehicle, it is very different from a regular diesel or petrol vehicle, there is much less wiring and equipment. There is just one battery. With this invention, we can eliminate that battery also. This can lead to path-breaking vehicle designs and efficiency improvements. The whole challenge around setting up additional infrastructure around charging also vanishes, allowing much higher adoption of electric vehicles."

Both now waited eagerly for Roshni to respond.

"You have literally done what every management consultant asks you **NOT** to do— *you have reinvented the wheel*" that is all Roshni could comment.

Chapter 4

The War Room

It was a Monday morning. Roshni carpooled to the office with some other staff of the company who lived in the same apartment. Apart from the environmental benefits of carpooling, this gave her an opportunity to understand the mindset of the staff on the ground and identify areas where she could help. Slow processes and lack of modern benefits were the two themes she would often hear on the way.

The Hampi meeting room was converted into a permanent war room for Project VC. The plan was to announce the partnership with Forest Automobiles to the media in a couple of weeks. The glass walls of the room, otherwise meant to showcase transparency in the workplace, were covered with posters, highlighting various products of RoadKing, to avoid any leakage of sensitive information related to the project.

There was a video conference planned with Mr. van Guard at 2 PM IST to discuss the plan ahead. Mr. Chopra, Gowda, Swamy and Roshni were supposed to attend the meeting.

The dinner held at the Chopra residence last Friday after Roshni was briefed about the project went way beyond the dinner to desserts and drinks covering technology, business and partnerships.

Swamy updated the group on the ongoing preparations for moving the project from lab to pilot scale. A small pilot plant was almost ready within the factory premises pending safety clearance. He also wanted to hire two more technologists and an equal number of lab technicians to oversee the pilot plant. He did not want to halt his team's focus on new research topics, hence, the need for more technologists.

"This is just the start. We can do a lot more with Artificial Intelligence and Nanotechnology. I don't want my team to lose steam."

Swamy also sounded cautious about sharing the details of his research with Forest unless all the agreements were in place. Deep inside, sharing his research with non-participants did not come naturally to him or, rather, to any researcher. If it were for him, he would have wanted to launch the project solo without any partnerships. But it was not only his decision to make.

Gowda spoke at length over dessert about the various legal clearances that would be required from government as well as non-governmental agencies as they progressed to the pilot phase and beyond. From the pollution control board to the electricity board to environmental control and even social impact.

"We will also have to negotiate the terms of agreement with Forest and draft corresponding clauses."

They moved over to the terrace for the final round of drinks. From a business perspective, the focus was to have an immediate and medium-term plan. Mr. Chopra never believed in having long terms plans. That was something he learnt from his father.

"You should have long-term vision, not long-term plan. Always plan for the immediate and medium term. And when you reach the medium term, again plan for the next immediate and medium term. This is how you achieve the long-term vision. There are many variables in business that keep changing and new variables keep adding, so there is no point having a long-term plan." He had often heard his father say that to his staff.

It was decided that Roshni would lead the overall project till the time of the product launch. Her immediate focus would be to finalize the details of the partnership with Forest Auto and oversee the pilot manufacturing unit towards the release of the final product in time for the global auto expo to be held in Delhi in six months.

"Any questions, Roshni?" asked Mr. Chopra.

Roshni was overwhelmed by the amount of information that she had to digest in the day since she first got to know about Project VC. She was frenetically making notes throughout the day. Some written, some mental. There were many questions she had noted for herself to research on, but there was one she wanted to ask now.

"Why do we need to partner with Forest? Wouldn't it be better for us if we go solo?"

Swamy's eyes shone on hearing this question. Someone thought like him.

But that was Gowda's question to answer, as he was the one who first suggested the partnership.

"There are multiple reasons. The foremost, for me, is hedging our risks, as I have already cautioned earlier. Second is the GTM strategy, that is, the Go To Market strategy. We are building a never-seen-before product. We need to know our product and its application and its limitations. Our product is intended for use in another product. The market needs working proof for every new product. And just the proof of concept is not enough. With Forest as a partner, we can showcase a new automobile, which uses the new tyre. If that product hits the market, there is no better proof of it working. And if that works, we will never look back. In addition, the partnership with Forest will allow us to learn a lot more through the interactions of our tyre with the new automobile design and allow us to make modifications. In effect, our GTM would be much faster and much impactful. A poorly executed GTM can kill the best of products."

Mr. Chopra added, "Also, our partnership with Forest will be mutually beneficial. They will get a one-year exclusive contract to use our technology to launch their vehicle and take a lead in the market. After the first year, we will be free to commercialize the technology with other partners."

Forest Auto GmbH was one of the oldest auto-manufacturing firms in Germany. Founded in 1910 and located in the state of Baden-Württemberg of Germany bordering France, it borrowed its name from the world-renowned Black Forest Range in the region, which also lends its name to the Black Forest cake or the original Black Forest gâteau.

With over a century of existence and experience, Forest was a strong player in the industry but had been facing the challenge of fierce competition from Chinese auto manufacturers and the threat of electric vehicles, of late. They were already late to the electric bandwagon and were looking at anything that would give them a lead.

Mr. van Guard, Head of International Business at Forest had known Mr. Chopra for over a decade now, having first met him at an Indo-German Business Partnership event organized by the Confederation of Indian Industries in Berlin. They kept in touch and kept bumping into each other at conferences and business events, always promising each other of an opportunity to work together.

When Gowda first suggested finding a partner for Project VC, several names cropped up in the mind of Mr. Chopra. He zeroed upon Forest, realizing that they would be the most hungry to lap up something like this. Something that would give them a lead in the game. This would give RoadKing a strong negotiating power and also allow them to use the Forest brand to capitalize on the launch.

Once again, his decision was correct. As expected, Forest lapped up the proposal. Within a week, Mr. van Guard presented the proposal to his CEO and received an A2N or an Approval to Negotiate. They surely didn't want to let this go.

After the Friday dinner, Roshni spent most of her weekend reading nanotechnology trends and analyzing future business assessments of electric vehicles. She, once again, had to cancel her planned movie outing with her college friends. She was afraid that if this continued, she would soon be ostracized by her friends. She recalled the horrendous time she had adapting to the college culture and how some of these friends helped her settle down and brave the storm. She owed them an outing.

"*Next week, for sure,*" she convinced herself.

It was 1:30 PM and the team of four had gathered in the war room for a final briefing before the call with Forest Auto.

"As we agreed, I will initiate the call and then Roshni will lead. If there are any technology or legal questions, Swamy or Gowda would take it," reiterated Mr. Chopra.

Roshni was nervous and excited. In any other circumstance, it would take a seasoned business leader to lead a project of this magnitude. And here she was with just her degrees, internships, and over two months of experience. But then her father always had high expectations of his daughter. Right from school, he always wanted her to be competitive and not be complacent due to the luxuries she got at home. He wanted her to have the same hunger for success as the daughter of an ambitious middle-class employee of his company who would dream of a better future through education.

As she grew and faced the world, she realized that the protected environment that she grew up in would never let her compete with the middle-class hunger, but she could make it up with her balanced approach and attention to detail. Those years in engineering school made her learn a lot and helped her recognize her potential and personality. But that didn't come easy. It was a tough ride. An unforgettable experience in many ways. She reminded herself to call her friends to apologize and plan an outing this coming weekend.

"Hallo, Herr van Guard," greeted Mr. Chopra in German.

"Namaasstey, Chopra jee," replied Mr. van Guard.

In the next 30 minutes, after Mr. Chopra formally introduced Roshni, she gave an update on the project status in terms of technology, business partnerships and regulatory requirements.

She had created a slide deck properly explaining the next steps with the clear breakup of responsibilities and a SWAT analysis. There was a slide on timelines; there was a slide on the various stakeholders; there was a slide on the business environment and competition; there was also a slide on the sources for the information on these slides.

Mr. Chopra, who generally did not believe in slides, was thoroughly impressed by the clarity provided by the slide deck and the plan for the future. His decision to let Roshni lead this once seemed to have got a good start, but there was still a long way to go.

"Thank you, Roshni. It was very well articulated. I am looking forward to working with you. From Forest, I will lead this partnership and will be supported by our head of R&D," said Mr. van Guard.

He then addressed her father. "Mr. Chopra, I would like to once again thank you for the opportunity to partner. What you have is a game-changing technology. Our R&D and Technology teams have vetted the technology details you have provided and are amazed and excited about the prospects of this new technology. According to them, it has the potential to revolutionize the automobile industry. We have created a core group of our best employees from the technology, R&D and Design teams, which have already started working on a new concept car design incorporating the new tyre technology. This will truly be the car of the future.

Our R&D Head and I would like to visit your premises in approximately a month's time to survey the pilot plant and spend time with your technology team to discuss further scope for development. At that time, we can also make a public announcement about the technology and our partnership.

In the meanwhile, I would suggest that we get the contracts and agreements done to ensure that we have all the legal formalities in place. I will share our NDA and form agreements for your legal team to review. As agreed, we will get into a one-year exclusive technology licensing agreement. I had just one question for you. We, at Forest, have a very strong IP Department."

The four in the Hampi room looked at each other. Mr. van Guard could sense the perplexity on their faces through the video screen.

"I mean Intellectual Property, you know patents and all. We would like to ensure that the technology is protected and we have an IP sharing clause in the agreements. I am assuming you have filed patents on the technology."

All eyes were on Gowda as all they could sense was that it was probably a legal question.

"Yes, we have asked our trademark attorney to file a provisional patent with the Chennai patent office," clarified Gowda.

Roshni thought she should have considered the concept of technology protection in her research. It never crossed her mind. Although she had no clue how patents worked, it definitely seemed important in the context.

She was wondering if that should go in the "threat" or "opportunity" quadrant of her SWAT analysis.

Chapter 5

Is Patent and Trademark the Same Thing?

The movie turned out to be a letdown. Roshni and her friends were laughing hard at the missing humour in the supposed comedy as they exited the cinema theatre. Even the big star cast and exotic foreign locales could not save it. It would sure feature in the list of most expensive box office duds.

Roshni was enjoying her time out. It had been ages since she watched a movie in a theatre with friends. Her only form of entertainment in the last few months and the months before that was watching shows on *Netflix*. She was a sucker for murder mysteries. From *Sherlock* to *Shetland* to *Elementary* to *How to Get Away with a Murder*, she had seen it all, thirty minutes at a time. Thirty minutes was her rule to avoid getting in the binge-watching trap! She would always set an alarm of thirty minutes while starting and would definitely stop with the alarm, no matter how intriguing the mystery was or how close it might be from being solved.

She had personally called all her friends and planned the outing. The movie and the dinner place were both her choices. She hoped the dinner place turned out better. She was glad that all of them except Trisha could make it for the evening. Although they were all connected on a WhatsApp group, getting updates by the hour, it was great to meet them in person and hear the same updates live.

Ganesh was taking a sabbatical from work and flying off next week with his girlfriend for a month-long hitchhiking trip across Europe.

"How cool is that?" Roshni thought. But that was not something she could even dream of doing for now with or without a girlfriend or boyfriend. Her next many months were going to be dedicated to Project VC. "Very Cruel" would have been a better expansion for VC.

Arpita was getting married in three months. Her fiancée, currently in Mumbai, was actively looking for a job in Bangalore to move in after marriage. Roshni offered to share his profile in her local alumni network and provide some connects. The girls made some big shopping plans and discussed venues for the bachelorette party.

She would be buried in Project VC in three months. It would be great if she got a day off for the wedding. Anything beyond that would need a miracle.

And Tanya was just happy as always. She was working with an interior design firm after graduating with her degree in architecture. Some of the snaps she had shared on WhatsApp of her home designs looked fabulous.

There is so much colour and creativity in her job. I wish we could at least make yellow and red tyres!

"Enough of VC!" Roshni cursed herself. "I am here to enjoy with my friends and take a break from VC. And VC is not so bad after all."

Trisha's absence was compensated for by Tanya's friend Krish. Tanya had texted on the WhatsApp group that she wanted to bring along her new boyfriend. Everyone agreed after they counted and confirmed with Tanya that this was her sixth boyfriend since the most famous first one in college. No one was complaining though!

The group settled on a table at the terrace of a recently opened Pan-Asian restaurant. Roshni had selected the place based on some great reviews from her carpool mates.

None of them had met Krish before. Even Tanya had known him for just over a month when she started working on the interiors for his office. She was impressed by his clarity on what he wanted the office to look like and the ease with which he drew the rough design sketches on paper. That didn't come easy to most. His designs and ideas were both bold and innovative.

"So Krish, tell us about yourself," asked Arpita almost in an 'interviewing for a job' tone.

Krish had been quiet most of the time. but he didn't seem to be the shy or introvert type. He was more the type who waited for their turn to speak rather than competing to speak. And when he spoke, one wanted to listen more. There was a scent of experience and a hint of wisdom in his words.

"Since you asked in an interviewish tone, I will answer the same way," Krish smiled. "My full name is Krishnaswamy Abhishekam, but I don't want any of you to remember that. I go by Krish. I have lived across the country as my father kept moving for jobs. From Assam to Himachal to Gujarat and Mumbai. I have been in Bangalore for the last 10 years. Can't imagine living anywhere else now."

"There is something you and Krish have in common, Roshni," interrupted Tanya. "He is also an entrepreneur."

"Don't dig at me, Tanya. I am no entrepreneur. I am working for my father. I get a monthly salary, and my father is a tough boss, he can fire me anytime! Although I would say I like my job for now."

Entrepreneur! Lived across places! That's where the experience and wisdom is coming from.

"Entrepreneur, wow! Let me guess; you are into software and run an IT consulting firm?" that was Ganesh.

"Well, I get that a lot and if it is some uncle or aunty, I let them have it. It is much easier to get away being a software engineer in Bangalore. You don't have to explain what you do. But actually, I am not into IT, I am into IP. Now, do you want to take another guess Ganesh at what IP stands for?" asked Krish in a 'giving it back' tone.

"Ohh, IP, you mean Intellectual Property, patents and all," Roshni immediately replied as if answering a question in a buzzer round of a quiz, repeating what she had heard the previous day from Mr. van Guard in the call.

"Now, that's a rare one," Krish stared at Roshni, seeming to have found a match.

"OK, but what exactly do you do? Let me guess again, you are a lawyer?" Ganesh seemed to be getting a little irritated.

"It's just not your day, Ganesh. Stop guessing. If your girlfriend calls you today and asks you 'Guess what special I am planning for our first night in Paris?', do not answer. You might get it wrong and ruin your Europe trip even before it starts."

That was savage but surely a good comeback. Experience, wisdom and wit.

"No, I'm not a lawyer. I have an engineering degree; I am a patent agent and an experienced patent professional; and I run a boutique IP consulting firm, providing support and services to corporates around IP-related matters."

Ganesh was sulking and avoided a response.

"I'm not sure what all that means, but I have a question. Is a patent and trademark the same thing? And wait... let me get this right. Can a trademark attorney... file a... patent?" Roshni completed the question with multiple pauses, trying to recall Gowda's response to van Guard's question on patents.

"No and preferably no. These are the quick answers to your two questions. I can give you a longer answer now or you can call me later."

"Hey, let's not talk about work here. You can call him later; I will give you his number," Tanya tried to change the topic sensing some tension. "Hey, Ganesh, where are you starting your Europe trip from?"

"Paris." Ganesh was still sulking.

The group spent the rest of the evening discussing a range of topics over dinner. Krish had many stories to share about his challenges of being an entrepreneur and explaining 'what he did' to his parents. Roshni was captivated by the subtle charm and the depth of content in Krish's storytelling style. At the end of the evening, she force volunteered Krish to walk her back to her apartment, which was a short walk from the mall. It seemed like a shorter walk than she thought it was.

****

That night, back in her apartment, Roshni tried to find answers to her questions online. She googled for "difference between patent and trademark" and got about 4,39,00,000 hits in 0.50 seconds.

Most of the results were from law firms and legal discussion portals. After browsing through the initial few results, the one thing she understood was that patents and trademarks fall under the broader umbrella of Intellectual Property or IP, which also included copyrights, designs, trade secrets and more.

Then she came across the WIPO webpage, which seemed to be a reliable source and some sort of a global IP agency. WIPO was World Intellectual Property Organization and it defined IP as:

Intellectual property (IP) refers to creations of the mind, such as inventions; literary and artistic works; designs; and symbols, names and images used in commerce.

Creations of mind? So, if I can create a superhero character that can fly, can I get a patent on that? Or would that be a trademark?

After reading some articles on the WIPO site, it was clear to her that patents and trademarks were two very different things. While patents related more to technical inventions, trademarks related to some sort of a sign or logo.

Then how can a trademark attorney file a patent?

"Preferably No" is what Krish had answered; does it mean that a trademark attorney can file a patent legally but may not have the required experience to do so?

I should ask Tanya for Krish's number and talk to him. It would anyways be nice to talk to him.

Chapter 6

What the Patent

An important aspect of leading a big project is managing people. And if the top members are as intellectually diverse as Swamy and Gowda, hearing becomes a key skill for the manager. Hearing is a rather underrated skill for people leaders. Patient hearing from a leader ensures the team members that their views are taken seriously and encourages them to speak fearlessly and resolve any differences.

Roshni, along with Swamy, had just completed surveying the latest machinery equipment installed in the pilot plant to manufacture tyre samples for a new design that the Forest technology team had shared.

They were now seated in a small meeting room in one corner of the pilot plant premises and were engaged in a mildly intense discussion. It was more of a telephone booth with two seats than a proper meeting room and the walls were not really soundproof. Ironic for a telephone booth! But the noise of the manufacturing machinery drowned their voices and there was no one around the room.

Swamy was disgruntled. He was vexed about what he termed as interferences by Forest's technical team in his research efforts. According to him, Project VC, which was now more commonly called pVC, was his and his team's brainchild and they had built it from scratch over many years.

"And now suddenly, the Forest guys try to barge in and suggest changes as if they know everything about it. Whatever new designs they are creating are based on the key technologies that we have developed. They should realize that and keep us informed about their efforts and also credit us. They have even filed some patents and added their team members as inventors on those patents. While I appreciate the freedom your father gave me, sometimes, I feel this is too revolutionary a technology for RoadKing. An enterprising startup would have handled it better. They would have more willingly followed the 'high-risk, high-reward' path rather than partnering with a larger firm who have more to gain from us than we do."

Swamy, like a true researcher, was possessive about his research. He wanted to own his research whether it hailed or failed. He was ready to face the consequences if it failed but also wanted to get the accolades for success. In any case, he was uncomfortable sharing it with anyone who was not involved since the beginning. It was Gowda's idea to bring a third party on board and he just tagged along.

But now when it was really happening, he was getting jittery about it.

Roshni had, by now, known Swamy enough to diagnose that he was having a bad day and that he didn't really mean most of what he was saying.

At the same time, she did not agree with Swamy's thoughts on collaboration. She was more with Gowda on this one. She believed in collaboration and she could see the value of that in the partnership with Forest.

It had been three months since she had begun leading the project and she was more than neck deep into it. She had not taken a day off since she last met her friends.

Last month, Mr. van Guard and Ms. Morgan, the Head of Research at Forest Auto, visited Bengaluru for a three-day official visit as planned.

The first day focused on business meetings. The one-year exclusivity clause was the most important aspect of the relationship for Forest. The one year was to start from the first commercial launch of the new concept vehicle by Forest using the pVC tyre. They wanted to hit the market with a bang with a never-seen-before vehicle and technology.

Forest had decades of experience and expertise around the design and manufacturing of automobiles. RoadKing wanted to capitalize upon that experience to pivot their technology into a strong and customizable product that would give them a head start over any future competition that may arise. RoadKing also wanted to leverage the Forest brand to get higher acceptability and visibility for their product. They were building a new category here and could use everything to get a solid start.

The second day was dedicated to the technology. Ms. Morgan had worked with Forest for over 25 years and was currently heading their research efforts. This was her first trip to India. Before the trip, she had done extensive study of the technical materials as well as the best food options in Bengaluru. She was all praise for Swamy and team for the innovative technology and had some great insights on how they could help advance the technology further through the use of Artificial Intelligence. Her team was working on remote monitoring and self-healing aspects of automobile components, and there could be some strong synergies between the pVC concept and their research. She had a marathon lunch-to-dinner meeting with Swamy and team, discussing her thoughts and brainstorming on immediate research and development topics. They ended with a prioritized list of new projects to initiate in the days to come.

There was also a one-hour virtual session on the Forest IP process conducted by Mr. Geert, IP Head at Forest. The session covered the basics of IP and the step-by-step process of idea to patent followed by Forest.

"We, at Forest, have a very strong IP Department," Mr. van Guard had previously stated.

On the last day of the visit, a press conference was organized to announce the official technology and business partnership between RoadKing and Forest Auto. Apart from some regular collaboration announcements, the press was also informed that RoadKing was working on a revolutionary new technology and collaborating with Forest to commercialize the technology in global markets. No details on the technology were divulged except that it relates to advancement in electric vehicles with a "more to follow" teaser. The tentative launch was scheduled for the global auto expo in another six months.

The news captured the attention of the domestic automobile industry and was covered by leading print and online media houses. There was a buzz around the possible revolutionary technology. In a rush for racy headlines, many media houses added a pinch of nationalism to the announcement. Some of the headlines read:

"Indian firm to announce revolutionary new technology in the EV space."

"Can India lead the future of EVs? RoadKing may have a clue."

"Can India produce the Tesla of the East?"

Most of the predictions were around a new battery technology or an electric three-wheeler. RoadKing received various follow-up media enquiries and Roshni even appeared for a few interviews on business channels and in newspapers. She had to repeatedly use the phrase "neither confirm nor deny" in all those interviews to fend off questions relating to the revolutionary technology.

The Forest team made a customary visit to the Taj Mahal over the weekend before taking the return flight back home.

For Roshni, the key learning from the visit was the potential for "innovation through collaboration" or co-innovation. Although it sounded like a modern innovation concept that might be taught in business schools, it had been around for long. During the middle ages, philosophers and explorers travelled across continents, learning new ideas, enriching, and adapting them to different cultures and geographies.

In the current global environment, with so much technological research happening, it would be professionally immature to innovate in silos. You never know what you are missing unless you go out and explore through collaboration. Focus on your strength and amplify it through collaboration. That was Roshni's approach to collaboration. But that needed an open mindset and willingness to give and take, learn and share.

RoadKing had a lot to benefit from the expertise that Forest brought to the table. And that was why she differed from Swamy in that telephone booth discussion.

Roshni tried to explain her viewpoint to Swamy and convince him of the benefits. She also assured him that she would talk to Ms. Morgan and convey some of his reservations to her.

Their discussion was abruptly interrupted by Sumitha, Mr. Chopra's admin executive who barged into the room without the courtesy of knocking and being totally unapologetic about it.

"I have been trying to contact both of you over the phone, but the network here is patchy. So I myself came running. Mr. Chopra wants you both in the boardroom immediately. Mr. Gowda is already there. I don't know what it is, but it sure is urgent. Let's go. NOW."

Roshni had heard stories of her father's urgent meetings from some other senior staff but had never experienced it herself. *What could it be?* she wondered.

Some senior member exiting. Forest pulling out of the partnership. Some significant change in regulations. A rival new technology announced.

Her mind was racing with random thoughts. Whatever it was, she would get to know in a few minutes.

As soon as they moved out of the pilot plant premises, their phones reconnected to the network and started buzzing with multiple notifications of missed calls and messages.

Swamy still seemed miffed about the discussion they were having and seemed to be further annoyed that they had left it inconclusive. He slowed down while reading his messages and was left behind a few steps as Roshni and Sumitha paced ahead.

"I have an urgent call to make. You both go ahead. I will join soon!" he shouted from behind.

That sounded strange to Sumitha as she had never seen anyone delay an urgent meeting call by Mr. Chopra, but she didn't have the time to think about it.

Sumitha stayed outside as Roshni entered the boardroom. Mr. Chopra was walking around the room with his hands folded at the back and Gowda was sitting with his laptop. There was a piece of paper next to him that he was referring to as he was entering some keywords on Google.

It was a plush boardroom with rich furnishing and state-of-the-art conferencing equipment. Behind Mr. Chopra was a showcase of a multitude of awards received by RoadKing over the years for business excellence and technical innovation in the tyre-manufacturing industry.

Mr. Chopra gestured to the paper next to Gowda, asking Roshni to read the first paragraph aloud.

The paper was a formal document. While browsing through the headings, Roshni realized it was a legal notice and the letterhead was of a company named Future Sensors. Roshni started reading the first para aloud.

"Based on the announcement made by RoadKing in the press conference of June 11 and in subsequent media interactions, we at Future Sensors believe that there might be a possible case of patent infringement by RoadKing of Future Sensors' granted patents related to the application of sensors in tyres specifically designed for electric vehicles.

We are sharing the details of our patents. We would like you to revert with the details of your technology and assess the level of infringement, if any. In case of an infringement, you may consider this as a notice to cease and desist from manufacturing, using, promising to sell, selling and importing products that infringe. We invite you to discuss terms for a formal licensing agreement and a failure to do so may amount to a case of wilful infringement."

"Future Sensors? What is this company? Who is behind this? This sure is a conspiracy from some competitor of ours to slow us down. There has never been a patent infringement case in the domestic automobile tyre industry. We have always been cooperative with each other," fumed Mr. Chopra. He was infuriated more by the language used and the accusations made at his firm without any background or proof.

Swamy entered the room and could immediately sense the tension in the room and on the faces. Roshni handed the letter over to him to read.

Roshni pulled Gowda's laptop and started browsing through the search results on Google for "Future Sensors". As she opened the home page of the company and started reading about the company history, her face turned pale.

"It's a startup," Roshni almost whispered with a sense of despair concerning what she was about to say and then picked up her voice. "It's a startup," she repeated in a bolder voice, "a startup focusing on latest Artificial Intelligence based sensor technologies with a variety of applications in the automobile industry," she continued, faltering again, before ending her sentence, "and it is started and owned by Rocky Dandekar."

"Rocky Dandekar? Now, I understand." Mr. Chopra was bewildered. He seemed to have found some answers but was more infuriated than before.

Chapter 7

Back to College

The hall was packed with some standing at the back. The occasion was the annual freshers' debate. The venue was the institute auditorium. And the audience included the staff and the students. It was the most popular event at the institute. Every year, one male and one female student from the incoming batch were selected after the first trimester to battle it out in the debate. The selection was based on written essays and multiple rounds of interviews conducted by members of staff and the previous years' debate participants.

Roshni Chopra and Rocky Dandekar were the two selected students for the year. Roshni had enrolled for the Chemical Engineering programme while Rocky had joined the Computer Science department.

The topic for this year's debate was

"Should hostel rooms have tiered pricing with basic and higher levels of comforts?"

Rocky was speaking for the motion and Roshni, against it.

"We all come from different backgrounds, different economic status and different lifestyles. What is comfort for one could be a necessity for the other and what is luxury for one could be a comfort for the other. I may be happy living in a simple room with just a bed and a study table whereas my dear friend Ms. Roshni may need an air-conditioned room with a soft mattress on the bed because that is what she is used to. And she should get it if she can pay for it. Why not? I would even propose that the money generated from such a scheme could be used for student welfare such as high-speed internet in the hostels or more reading rooms in the library," started Rocky with his defence.

It was Roshni's turn. She had a good command over the language, which helped her get selected among the few girls in the new batch. However, a debate in front of such a big crowd was a first for her.

"We have all cleared the same entrance exam to secure a seat in this institute, we will all be studying in the same classes, and we will all be living together in this beautiful campus for the next four years. So, for the sake of equality, I would strongly propose that all students be provided with the same rooms with the same facilities. As my fellow debater opined, I may be used to air-conditioning and a softer bed and I can also afford to pay more to buy more comforts. However, I won't want to do that, as that may create a rift between my to-be friends and me. And I am here to make friends for life," started Roshni with a shade of naivety clearly visible in her statements. She had no clue of the trap she was getting into.

The debate veered back and forth between the two speakers for almost thirty minutes with Rocky coming back stronger every time and Roshni clearly losing the plot before the final blow came from Rocky.

"Roshni thinks we are all equals on this campus. Let's see."

"I have delivered newspapers, I have worked part time at McDonald's, I have taught tuitions to school kids, all along with managing my academics and household responsibilities. But let me guess, Ms. Roshni, all this while, you were sitting in your air-conditioned room, attending personalized online classes and taking breaks from your hectic studying schedule to go to the nearby mall in your chauffeur-driven Mercedes to watch a movie and pick up a McSomething burger from a McDonald's where someone like me would be serving you happily with dreams of making it big someday. How can we be equals?

Education sure is a great leveler. It has the potential to make our next generations equal, but we will never be equal. My past will always be a part of myself and I am proud of it. My kind have to walk a much farther distance in much harsher conditions to reach somewhere in life than your kind.

Even now, I am working on a YouTube channel to earn money to cover my expenses and you must be getting pocket money from your father. And by the way, when you say you can afford more comforts, it's not you but your father who can make you afford that. Get that straight first."

"But you say we are equals, so maybe I am missing something. I rest my case."

Rocky's closing remarks were followed by thunderous applause and whistles by the student sections. Roshni's attempt to come back was drowned in the applause.

Rocky won the debate hands down. Roshni was just not prepared for the onslaught in the debate and also in the days ahead on the campus.

That was the beginning of a fierce battle between the two that raged for the next four years of college life.

Rocky had a disdain for the privileged and always wanted to prove a point to them. They had it all and they wanted more with little effort. At the other end, the lesser privileged had to toil to even make ends meet. They only had the passion within them that kept them going.

And Roshni, for him, was the ideal representative of the privileged section of the society.

It was his aim in life to tilt the balances.

Rocky reigned in the first year. From the debate to academics to sports and social events, he was just cruising. He came from a tough but humble background, and the college atmosphere was a breeze for him. He had earned a scholarship, which took care of his fees. He ran a YouTube channel where he advised younger students from underprivileged backgrounds and shared tips and best practices on efficient studying techniques and how to crack entrance exams. His channel was getting popular and the advertising revenue was helping him make some money for his regular expenses.

On the other hand, Roshni had a disastrous first year. College and hostel life was her first real exposure to the world outside the comforts of home. She was known in the institute as "the daughter of a business tycoon", a tag she wanted to get rid of through her performance. She was a good student at school and did well in the entrance exams to secure a position for herself in the first attempt. But she was not at all emotionally and mentally prepared for college life.

She would often break down in her room after classes and had long calls with her mother who would tell her stories about her own humble upbringing in the villages of Punjab.

"It is neither your fault nor anything to be ashamed of that your father and grandfather worked hard to be able to afford the lifestyle we have. Their success should be aspirational for the likes of Rocky, and if he puts in the efforts now, he would definitely deserve the same success in the future. At the same time, it does not make your efforts any less. You are there to learn and contribute in your own way to make the world a better place."

Roshni's other anchor was Tanya, her roommate and her first real friend. She had joined the architecture department in the institute. Tanya came from a simple middle-class family, the type who would go to a luxury restaurant once a year for her birthday celebration and would share the dessert to keep the bill low.

Tanya was a great influence in helping Roshni settle down throughout the first year of college. She would always be by her side and would fight for her if anyone passed a nasty comment. She also taught Roshni some common college cuss words and how alcohol could help get rid of her stress sometimes.

All that eventually worked. By the end of the first year, Roshni was able to handle the situation and gel with the environment. She made some more friends and could focus on academics and other activities.

She was giving a better fight to Rocky in the second year although she had lost some ground in the first year. The "Rocky Vs. Roshni" rivalry was the talk of the campus. Be it academic supremacy or success in extracurricular activities, the top two positions were reserved for these two.

By the end of the second year, Roshni had almost made up for what she lost in the first year through sheer hard work and determination. And by the end of the third year, both were neck to neck.

As the fourth year began, the battle reached its peak. On stake was the institute gold medal for the best all-round student of the batch. There were only two contenders.

But college life isn't all about academics and extracurriculars. It is also about emotional sparks fashioned by a winged, naked, infant boy with a bow and arrows, yes, Cupid. Cupid works overtime in campuses and in strange ways.

Towards the end of the third year, through an unpredictable stroke of Cupid, Rocky and Tanya grew close to each other, as they were both involved in a pre-final year project. It was a very delicate balance for Tanya as she was still Roshni's best friend though no more her roommate. As Tanya got to know Rocky more, she could appreciate his viewpoint but also wanted him to understand how Roshni was right in her position.

Love bloomed for six months before Cupid changed his mood, resulting in a bitter breakup between the two. It was the middle of the final year by then and the whole affair and the following breakup diverted Rocky from his otherwise focused approach towards his fight with Roshni. On the other hand, Roshni continued her dedicated attitude to get rid of "the daughter of the business tycoon" tag.

Rocky always blamed Roshni for hatching the "love plot" with her best friend to divert his focus.

On their final day in the institute at the outgoing batch awards ceremony, Rocky and Roshni were seated next to each other. The chief guest was announcing the awards,

"The gold medal for the batch of 2010 for all-round achievement in the field of academics, sports and extracurricular goes to... Roshni Chopra."

Rocky was miffed to the core. There was thunderous applause as loud as it was on the freshers' debate day when Roshni had lost the debate to Rocky.

"This is not the end of it, Roshni" were the words of Rocky, as Roshni stood up and moved to the podium. That was the last Roshni saw or heard of Rocky.

Chapter 8

Patent Family is Asexual

"Rocky Dandekar? Now, I understand."

Mr. Chopra was bewildered. He seemed to have found some answers but was more infuriated than before.

In the boardroom, Roshni gave some context about her past with Rocky to Swamy and Gowda. Her father was aware of her clashes with Rocky during campus days. She never had long conversations with him on this topic as she had with her mother. In the short conversations she had with him, his only advice to her was "think like him".

"You have moved out of the confines of your home now. You will get exposed to people and circumstances you might never have faced or imagined before. Observe and learn from it. There is no immediate solution. It is going to be a process. and you will come out a smarter and matured person." Those were her father's words, which seemed like a sermon then but now, in hindsight, felt so true.

"But how did he even get to know about the technology? Could there be someone from inside involved?" wondered Gowda

"I don't think so. He is coming back at me. He had warned me on the last day at college. I never took it seriously but always had it somewhere at the back of my mind. He is taking the fight to the next level."

"And he doesn't need to know the details of the technology. The notice is based on the announcements made in the press meet," opined Swamy.

"Roshni, you are leading this project. When I chose this as a challenge for you, I was expecting unpredicted hurdles although a patent infringement was not one. This is not something I have myself ever faced. But I want you to handle this and get us out of this unscathed. I would have handled it in my own way, but I leave it to you how you want to handle it. And above all, it is personal for you. Rocky is coming for you through this case. You have given it back to him once; you can give it back to him again." Mr. Chopra had, by now, regained his composure.

It was a patent-related matter and Roshni knew just the guy to talk to.

"Thanks, Dad. I'm up for it. Let me call someone I know who can help and set up a meeting," Roshni searched for a number in her contacts and made a call.

"Hi, Krish, this is Roshni, Tanya's friend. Hope you remember me."

"Hey, sure I do. Hi, Roshni. How are you?"

"I am good. Thanks. Do you have time for a quick chat?"

"Yeah. I am actually in the middle of lunch, which is in the middle of a training session. So, if it's real quick, sure."

"Yeah, it'll be quick. I am in my office with our leadership team. There is an urgent issue that has come up, and it relates to IP. I was wondering if we could meet and get your guidance on how to address it. Can you come over today?"

"Okay. I think I know the RoadKing office, and actually, I'm not far from it. I can be there by 5:00 PM. Would that work?"

"Sure, see you then."

Later in the day, Krish was in the boardroom at the RoadKing office along with Roshni, Gowda, Swamy and Mr. Chopra. Roshni handed the notice received from Future Sensors to Krish and gave him a business and technical context without getting into her personal history with the founder. Swamy was about to enthusiastically start explaining the technology before Krish interrupted.

"I have heard of Future Sensors. They are known in the IP world as a smart technology startup who has handled their IP strategy very well. They have also successfully licensed their patents on electric vehicle battery sensors to a major automobile manufacturer. Anyways, we will come to that later. So you think you have a revolutionary technology related to electric vehicles. Good for you. But don't tell me any more without signing an NDA."

"Let's sign an NDA now? We have two weeks' time to reply to Future. I don't want to delay it. We need to have this discussion initiated. Mr. Gowda is our legal head. Mr. Gowda, can we sign an NDA now?" Roshni seemed to be in a serious hurry.

Gowda quickly sourced a copy of their standard NDA, and Krish emailed a copy of his standard service agreement. Both documents were printed, reviewed and signed. Krish was officially on boarded as a service provider in a matter of few minutes.

Krish was wondering how strange it was that, sometimes, it took companies months to think about the need for IP and sign an agreement after multiple follow-ups and how the same was done now in a matter of minutes due to an emergency situation. But that is human nature. Don't we keep avoiding that regular health checkup for weeks and then suddenly leave everything aside and rush to a hospital if someone we know suffers an unexpected heart attack?

Necessity may be the mother of invention, but fear sure is the father of protection.

Swamy then went on to explain the details of the technology with the same enthusiasm as he did to Roshni a few months back.

"That sounds like a great technology. Have you done a prior art search or a landscape analysis?"

The clueless looks on the four faces in the room made Krish realize he had gone a bit too far. He stepped back and asked a simpler question.

"Have you filed a patent?"

"We have filed a provisional patent. I always wanted to file more patents around the technology but didn't get the budget to do so. While Mr. Chopra always gave me a free hand in my research efforts, patent fell under the legal domain and, hence, the decision was Gowda's," added Swamy in a *"I told them so"* tone.

"Yes. Our trademark attorney filed a provisional patent for us. That seemed like a good strategy to have some protection while keeping the cost low," defended Gowda.

Krish looked at Roshni, now realizing the source of the question she had asked him that evening at the outing with her friends.

"Mr. Gowda, would you go to a dentist if you are having vision problems?" questioned Krish.

"No."

"And will you go to a CA if you want to build a house?"

"Not at all. I know what you are getting at. But we have been working with this trademark attorney for a long time, and we have a portfolio of trademarks that he manages. And doesn't it all fall under the common umbrella of what you call it... Intellectual Property?"

"Patents protect technical inventions whereas trademarks protect some sort of a sign or logo. Right, Krish?" Roshni pitched in, recalling her readings on the topic.

Mr. Chopra, who had been silently listening to the conversation all the while, leaned in with his thoughts.

"What I understood is that patents cost a lot of money, and the return on that investment is very uncertain. So, if I look at it from a business perspective, it does not make sense to me. It looks good on product brochures and marketing material to say that we have a patent, but beyond that, I do not see much value. And as a businessman, I know that business works through strategic partnerships and the whole idea of patenting goes against that. You are trying to exclude others rather than partnering with them."

"Sir, let me share my perspective on cost and partnering. Let's talk about costs first, if you don't have a patent, then the cost of protecting yourself if someone else asserts their patents against you may be much higher than the cost of filing patents upfront. Like it seems to be happening now with this notice. Plus, it is a common misconception that patents are costly. There are various strategies to manage your patenting costs, and the amount you spend should be commensurate to the value you are expecting in return."

"Secondly, regarding your point about partnership, no partnership happens without negotiations. You would know more about it than me. Having a patent gives you stronger control over your technology and, hence, an advantage at the negotiating table. As a businessman, you would agree that the best negotiation happens when each party negotiates on their strength."

It was one of those few occasions when Mr. Chopra did not have a response or a counterargument nor did anybody else in the room. They were all listening to Krish with the same interest as final year students paying attention to pre-placement talks by companies coming with job offers to college campuses.

"Can I have a look at the provisional application filed? In the meanwhile, let me open my laptop and check out the patents of Future Sensors," Krish continued.

Gowda stepped out of the room to fetch the file with provisional patent documents, and Krish opened up his laptop and logged into a patent search portal.

"The first thing I ask my clients or try to understand from them is why do they need to file patents? There are various reasons for filing patents; it could be to protect a new technology, to defend yourself against potential lawsuits, to showcase patent pending status for investments or marketing or even to avail some government grants.

According to me, the purest reason for filing patents is to protect your invention, the creations of your mind. So that you can get the returns on your creative and financial investments. It is a sort of insurance on your investment. And in your case, you have fabulous technology. It is in your interest to create a strong portfolio of patents around the technology."

As the patent database loaded, Krish entered the patent numbers mentioned in the notice from Future Sensors and started browsing through the results.

"Future seems to have a good portfolio of patents. The three families they have referred to in the notice each have a granted patent in the US and India."

"Families?" Swamy enquired.

Krish smiled when Swamy asked the question. He loved answering this question in his sessions.

"Thanks for asking. Yes, patents have a family. There is a mother patent and a father patent; both come together, switch off the lights and have baby patents. And the patent family lives happily ever after."

Nobody was amused except Krish himself. The answer didn't get the response that he generally got in his sessions, which were more casual and fun. He realized that the setting here was different. But he continued.

"Ok. Not really, that was a joke. Maybe a bad joke. But if you think of it, what I explained was an example of sexual reproduction. A patent family is more an example of asexual reproduction, like in amoeba, if you recall your grade 7 biology. A patent family starts with the first patent filed in a country. Beyond that, following legal guidelines of various countries, the same idea can be filed for patents in multiple countries. You may decide which countries you want to file in, depending on your budget, business strategy and market for your products. All the patents for the same idea filed in different countries constitute a patent family."

Gowda walked back in the room and handed over a file to Krish, which was titled "RoadKing Provisional Patent".

"I would also like to add that after our partnership with Forest Auto, they have been handling the patenting part. They have an experienced in-house IP team," clarified Gowda as he handed the file over to Krish.

"They have filed seven more patents on the core idea and its modifications and application in an automobile. They have also included some of their employees as inventors on those patents," added Swamy clearly showing his discomfort at this fact.

As Krish was going through the contents of the file, Roshni asked a follow-up question on patent families.

"Shouldn't there be a single world patent? Isn't it costly and inconvenient to file in so many countries?"

"I was waiting for that question. 87% of the time when I explain the concept of patent families, this comes up as a follow-up question. Should there be a single world patent? Maybe yes. Is there a single world patent? Definitely no. By the way, that 87% was a fake fact.

Patent law varies across countries, and each country would like to examine every patent application before it allows or rejects the patent. Hence, you do need to file separately in each country where you need protection. Think of it as a driving licence. Each country has some differences although the core concept remains the same. So, like with humans, proper family planning is pertinent for patents. This is where either the cost can spiral or vital protection may be lost if not planned properly.

Having said that, there are some mechanisms, which help you file a single application for multiple countries initially and decide later which countries you want to file in further. It buys you time to take a final decision and make the investment. There is PCT, the Patent Cooperation Treaty, which covers all major countries in the world, there is the European Patent Office for Europe, and there is ARIPO for Africa."

"And on what basis do they allow or reject an application?" Roshni continued with her questioning.

"The three main criteria for patentability are novelty, non-obviousness and utility. Now, these criteria may sound self-explanatory, as in novelty means something that is new or never done before, non-obvious means something that is not obvious to a person skilled in the art, and utility means that the idea should have valid use. However, from a legal perspective, they are very subjective and require detailed analysis and, hence, are better left to the professionals."

"So, what do you suggest as next steps?" asked Mr. Chopra. He was clearly uncomfortable in the situation. He was not able to come on terms with the fact that a patent, something he considered very trivial, could be a threat to his business.

"Can you share copies of the patents filed by Forest and set up a call with the Forest IP team? I would like to understand their approach and go through the patents they have filed. That will help me understand your overall standing. I will then need to do a detailed study of the technology space and of the Future patents to understand the actual level of threat and plan a response strategy. Based on the first look at the FS patents and your technology, I must say that it seems like FS has created a smart patent portfolio with an intention to outsmart you. And these patents were filed almost 2 years back. Is there a possibility that they knew you were working on such a technology?"

"The only people aware of this technology two years back would be Swamy and his team members," reasoned Roshni.

"I can vouch for my team members."

"Let's hold that for now. That is for you to investigate. The only good news, for now, is that you have a few patents including the provisional, although poorly drafted by a trademark attorney. However, just one provisional patent does not do justice for the revolutionary technology that you have. I would term it as strategic hara-kiri. I will have to go through the additional patents filed by Forest and what they cover. And the bad news is that FS has a strong patent portfolio, which can help them can get an injunction and stop you from selling your product if they can prove a potential infringement."

"Let's move fast on this, Krish. Please start your analysis. I will coordinate with you on the next steps." Roshni was ready to take this head on.

Chapter 9

Can She Do It?

The cafeteria at the RoadKing office was rather modest as compared to the swanky cafeterias generally seen in the other IT offices in Bangalore. The ambience was traditional and the food was more payasam than pasta.

Gowda and Swamy, irrespective of their differences, would often join for lunch. This gave them a good opportunity to catch up on the status of the research and legal aspects of ongoing projects. On lighter days, they would also talk about the eccentricities of their boss and how they both had learnt to manage him.

But this day was anything but light. The notice from Future Sensors the previous day had put them in an awkward position. It had put a sudden brake on the otherwise fast-paced progress they were making on pVC. They had no idea what the impact of the notice in the short and medium term could be.

Gowda had extensive knowledge and exposure on legal matters, but he had never before handled an Intellectual Property matter except for routine trademark filings for RoadKing with the help of their external trademark attorney.

Swamy had some exposure to patents as an inventor in his previous employment and education, but his participation was restricted to the technical disclosure aspect. He rarely dabbled in the legal aspects of filing, except for signing some forms and had no clue of litigation aspects. He didn't even know how many of his patents were granted.

The meeting with Krish threw some light on their options, although not much of it seemed to be positive.

"When we started this project, we had thought of all challenges we might face—technology, cost, regulations, manufacturing—but never imagined that a patent litigation could be a threat; it wasn't even on Roshni's fancy SWOT analysis slide," grumbled Gowda

"Yes, this is a new one for us and not only for us, for the industry. As Mr. Chopra said, this might be the first patent infringement case in the domestic industry. Do you think that Krish guy can handle this? Shall we put faith in him or hire someone more experienced? He looks young and smart, but matters like these need more grey hair."

"He seemed to have good knowledge of the subject. And Roshni invited him and hired him immediately. She is leading the whole project, so let her make the decision. On that point, do you think even she can handle this situation? She sure is a fast learner but has zero experience on such matters. It is one thing to lead a project with support from experienced mentors, and it is totally another to handle a crisis of this magnitude. I don't think she has it in her. We might further jeopardize the situation by leaving it to her."

Before Swamy could respond, he saw an unexpected visitor to the cafeteria walking in behind Gowda. He immediately stood up and welcomed his boss.

Both were surprised as Mr. Chopra, who rarely came to the cafeteria, walked in and joined them at their table. He could guess the topic of discussion, going by their hushed tone and the rather disturbed look on their faces.

"We can't allow a small startup to disrupt our investments. We have put so much time, money and effort into this." Gowda was trying to keep his voice low.

"Do you know the meaning of the word "disrupt"? Disruption happens unexpectedly, it happens to you when you are not prepared. If you are prepared, no one can disrupt you. What we are trying to do with our research is to disrupt the electric vehicle industry because the industry is not prepared for such an innovation. Similarly, what Future Sensors is trying to do is to disrupt us legally with the help of their patents because we are not prepared for this scenario. We have good technology to disrupt but maybe not the legal discipline and foresightedness to protect us from being disrupted." Swamy was never the one to shy away from giving it back to Gowda

Gowda was taken aback. Somewhere inside, he realized that this was a legal matter and he needed to take responsibility.

"How do we handle something like this? Do you think you can use your chairmanship of the Tyre Manufacturers' Association to put some pressure on this company?" suggested Swamy to Mr. Chopra.

"You both know well, I am not the one to take undue advantages. My position at the manufacturing association is to upgrade the overall industry and benefit the members, not to resolve my personal business problems. We have to think of other solutions, but before that, we need to better understand the problem, which I don't think any of us know well. As of now, the first thing we need to ensure is that this does not leak out to the media. If this becomes public, it can have a severe negative impact on our stock and business activities."

For the other staff having lunch in the cafeteria, seeing the three big guns sitting together in the corner was nothing less than a celebrity-spotting coup. For some, this was perfect fodder for gossip. Some even quietly took pictures with their smartphones and sent to their personal chat groups with titles like "something's cooking in the cafeteria". Others could figure out that it was a rather serious matter and kept their distance from that corner.

"Also, as we all know now, this case is more out of vengeance than business or legal considerations. We have to keep that in mind while planning our strategy. What is our legal position?" Mr. Chopra questioned Gowda.

"I must say, I am nervous. This is as unchartered territory for us as the Project VC itself. I have no idea how strong a case we have if we take it to the courts. I will need some legal advice on the matter. But the case may surely drag for years, delaying our launch and also causing business damage. Our best option would be to explore out-of-court settlement?"

"Do you think Roshni can handle it?" Mr. Chopra reversed the questioned to the two.

"We were discussing this just as you entered. And we are rather unsure."

"I am not sure too, but even we have zero exposure to handle this situation. At the same time, I am equally unsure if our old world minds can handle this. Our approach might make matters more complicated. Roshni may not have the experience, but at least she has a modern outlook and mindset to handle this. And it seems like she also has some good contacts."

"And this would be her real challenge. The true grit of a leader comes out in handling unexpected challenges. Let her prove whether she is worthy of handling the firm in the future. Let her prove her inheritance is legit."

"So you are dating my ex now? I had never thought it will come down to this!" Tanya teased Roshni on the phone.

"To be honest, I had myself never thought so, but things happen. I have learnt a lot from him."

"This is so interesting. I want to know the whole story."

"It is a long story. Will need a full night out, and I don't see that happening anytime soon."

"Hmmm, how's your super-urgent, highly-secretive project going?"

"Super busy and getting more complicated. That reminds me, I need to go now, I have to meet Krish at his office."

"Okkk... I have a special connect with that office. Say my hello to him; it's been a while since we swiped left."

An hour later, Roshni was at Krish's office. Being a Sunday, the office was empty. Roshni had brought along some sandwiches and coffee.

This was the office that Tanya was involved in designing and where she had first met Krish during the design planning. It was a small but smartly planned office, more like a studio office. There were ten work desks on one side in a honeycomb arrangement, an open area in the middle with beanbags around, coffee and snacks stalls and four meeting rooms, including a video conferencing room on the other side.

She was impressed by his clarity on what he wanted the office to look like and the ease with which he drew the rough design sketches on paper.

They had settled on the beanbags in the central common area and were having a casual chat over food.

"So, I understand that you and Tanya are no longer a couple. WWW?"

"WWW?"

"What Went Wrong?"

"Ohh, nothing, I won't say it was a breakup breakup; we went around for some time and agreed that swipe left was the right thing to do."

Swipe left was the new term for the millennials to agree to move on without any bitter feelings.

"OK, coming to work, what do we need to present to our leadership team as a response to the notice?"

"I would first start with a review of all your filed patents, if they effectively cover the core technology and all possible variations. For technology as futuristic as yours and something that will have a market across the world, we need to have a strong portfolio of patents that covers all aspects of the technology."

"A web of patents," Roshni spoke with an animated voice and hands waving like a magician.

"I don't call it a web, as it gives a negative perception of trapping others. For me, a strong patent portfolio is like a fortress wall that shields you from any malicious attacks while allowing you to invite potential partners and collaborators inside your fort."

"Got it. So, a strong patent portfolio that protects us, but we will also need to know who can attack us. A patent landscape? Isn't that what you call it?"

"Exactly. You seem to be doing your homework well. A landscape would be very useful here. It will help us understand what else is happening in the space and who the active players are."

"Great. Let's do it then. I think I have done enough homework; it is now time to take the test, and for the first time in my life, I am so confident about taking the test."

"One more question. What exactly is a provisional patent? I have been hearing that a lot."

"A provisional patent, as the name suggests, is a provisionally filed patent to secure a priority date for the filing. It is generally done in rush situations when you may either be disclosing the idea in a public forum or discussing it with a client. In your case, neither applied, so it was not a good idea to file a provisional. Gowda just looked at it as an opportunity to delay costs and went for it. You should have filed a detailed set of patents for your technology. Also, a provisional needs to be followed by a full specification non-provisional application within 12 months of filing; else, you lose the priority date."

"This whole IP thing requires lots of strategic decisions at each step—where to file, what to file, when to file, I used to think of it as a set of rules and laws."

"It does. Glad you appreciate that. In today's world, innovating is not enough. You need to protect your innovations."

Krish and Roshni spent the next couple of hours debating and whiteboarding upon the various aspects of an IP strategy and a response outline to the Future Sensors' notice to present to the RoadKing leadership.

At the end of the session, they picked another cup of coffee each from the coffee machine and settled at the beanbags again.

"So how's your leadership trio taking this whole thing?"

"I must say they are caught totally unaware, something that's never before happened to them to this extent. So, I think they are a bit unnerved. I also have a feeling that they are looking up to me to handle this."

"You are doing great. I am sure you can handle this. And I am with you on this one."

"Thanks, Krish. I am counting on you."

"Any other office gossip?"

"Ohh yeah, I forgot to tell you, this is interesting. You know, Sumitha, Dad's admin in-charge?"

"Yeah, I think she was the one who escorted me to the board room the other day, when I visited your office."

"Yes, that's right. She has been around for a long time and knows everything that is going on in the company but, at the same time, she is very professional in avoiding any sort of gossip. But sometimes, she does open up to me. And after all this drama happened, she came over to me..."

"And?" Krish sounded interested.

"And she confessed that she has a strong intuition that Mr. Swamy is up to something rather unholy. The way he stopped to take the call while we were going for the meeting and some other things she noticed recently about him makes her feel so. And she thinks it may be related to the latest challenge we are facing though she doesn't know what exactly the challenge is about."

"And how did you respond?"

"I tried to reason with her that I don't think so. I believe Swamy is totally committed to us although, sometimes, he does get frustrated, there is nothing that gives me any reason to doubt him. She still believed in her intuition and suggested we wait for some time and reconnect on this."

"That's interesting. I will be watching this space," smiled Krish.

Chapter 10

Having a Team Is Not the Same As Having a Strategy

"Thanks, Mr. Gowda, for setting up the call. Hello, Mr. Geert, pleased to e-meet you."

Krish was sitting in his office connected with the RoadKing team and the Forest Auto team through video conferencing. The regular four from RoadKing were connected and from Forest, there was Mr. van Guard and Mr. Geert, the IP Head for Forest Auto connected from their offices in Germany.

"Hello, Krish. Nice to e-meet you too. I have heard great things about you and your firm from a friend of mine whose company is one of your clients," replied Mr. Geert.

"Thanks, I hope I live up to the praise. Mr. Gowda had shared with me the copies of the original provisional and the seven additional patents filed on the core technology and further developments through collaboration between RoadKing and Forest. I have gone through those and have also read in detail the three patents that Future Sensors has cited in its notice. Roshni and I had an in-depth discussion around the coverage of the patents and we would like to present some of our initial findings today. We also talked to some members of the technology teams at RoadKing and Forest. I will give a quick summary of our assessment till now and then we have a few questions for you, Mr. Geert."

"Sure, go ahead." Mr. Geert sounded very confident.

"Let's talk about technology first because any IP is a function of technology. Whenever I talk to scientists, researchers, product developers or inventors, the first thing I tell them is that almost 98% of the time, your idea, your product, your research or your invention would already be practised or invented before. It is unlikely to be groundbreaking."

"I totally disagree. I am 100% confident that no one has ever built or even thought of the idea of a battery housed in a tyre," Swami almost thundered.

"I also add a disclaimer immediately after that; this statistics of 98% is not to discourage you or demean your invention in any way. It means…"

"I agree with Krish," interrupted Mr. Geert in support of Krish "We, IP professionals, are exposed to unknown ideas and products on a daily level while searching and analyzing patents. The world of patents is full of amazing ideas, which are never commercialized and may never get to see the world beyond the patent files and gazettes. Inventors believe their ideas are completely novel, but most of the time, there is a similar patent, paper or publications sitting somewhere, which the world has not savoured. The world of patents is a treasure trove of great ideas. The more you read about ideas, the better connections your mind can make. And it can come up with new ideas. In fact, Albert Einstein worked in the patent office as an examiner, and he has even credited his job of a patent examiner as the fertile ground, where the seeds of his future research success were sown. However, it is also a fact that there are equal numbers of or even more nasty or useless patents, but let's focus on the positives."

"Thanks, Mr. Geert. That's exactly my point. By the way, I did not know about Einstein. That's very interesting; I will use it in my training sessions."

"Then what's the whole point of filing patents when 98% of it is already out there. Isn't that what you call prior art?" asked Mr. Chopra who, by now, had developed some interest in the topic of IP, something he had never before explored in his career.

"There is a difference, sir, and that is why I add the disclaimer. The 98% stat is not to discourage the inventors from inventing, rather to advise them to know the space before investing their time, money and effort. A proper patent analysis can help them understand where to focus the research efforts. 98%

of basic concepts may have been developed, but it does not mean that you cannot modify it or come up with a new use case or identify some limitations and solve for it. There are many possibilities. To give you an example, QR code as a concept was developed by a subsidiary of Toyota Motors to track vehicles' parts in their manufacturing facility more than two decades back, and today, we use the same humble QR code in a variety of applications, and there are thousands of patents filed around it."

"Oh, that's interesting, I didn't know about the QR code example. I will use it for my trainings now," Mr. Geert immediately claimed the returned favour.

"Coming back to the original question from Mr. Swamy, I would probably agree with you. As I did not find a similar patent or publication, so your idea probably is in the remaining 2%. I must say, the more I read about the technology, the more fascinated I was by it. Kudos to the RoadKing research team. But there are hundreds of minds around the world working on solving the same problem, so it is always important to not just innovate but also protect your innovations."

Swamy beamed with pride under a sense of vindication.

"And we did that. We did file a provisional early in the process." Gowda wanted at least some part of the vindication

"You did but you approached the filing more as a formality than a plan. Filing a provisional patent was not the best strategy in your case and that too one that was drafted by a trademark attorney. There are nuances of drafting and filing a patent application and hence it is best left to the right professionals. For a technology as path breaking as yours, you needed a much broader IP strategy which you never had and that's where you lost the advantage of your investment on innovation."

"Filing a patent or a set of patents need some analysis and discussion with the inventors and business to understand what the technology is, where the innovations lie, what are the potential use cases and what could be future modifications and applications. So apart from understanding the current technology you also need to understand how could other players create a work around or circumvent your technology and that should be covered in the patents. You also need to understand what could be different variations of the components and sub-components used."

"The patents you have filed including the ones filed by the Forest team are what I call plain Vanilla patents. They cover the very basic aspects of the technology and lack technological research and imagination that is very important for drafting a strong patent and I repeat this, more so for technology as unique as yours."

"We have always been proud of our IP team in Forest" Mr. van Guard who was mostly quiet pitched in "and from what I understood from Geert here is that our patents cover the core technology well so where exactly are the Future Sensors patents hurting us?"

"The patents that you have filed cover the core technology." Krish stood up as he spoke and moved towards the whiteboard in the room and started drawing a tyre and marked various sections. "It includes modifications in the material of the tyre, placement of the layers within the tyre, the self-charging of the tyre through interaction with the surface of movement. The patents filed later by Forest also cover further implementation of the technology in a vehicle."

At this point, Roshni joined Krish at the whiteboard, drew a partial car over the tyre showing the dashboard, and included some Wi-Fi-type symbol marks indicating communication between the tyre and the car in the diagram.

"Ok, so I tried to do what Krish is rightfully accusing us of not doing," Roshni started speaking as she completed the drawing.

"I spoke to our team members in research and business across RoadKing and Forest teams and collected some additional information trying to go a little deeper and broader into the application of our technology. From what I understood, when our tyres are installed in a vehicle, they interface with various sensors and onboard diagnostic components to regularly collect data around temperature, pressure, speed, etc. to regulate the charging levels.

In our patents, we have not elaborated on the sensors. At the time of filing the patents, we assumed that the regular sensors would work. However, when we extended the implementation beyond our labs to the pilot plant, we realized that in place of the regular sensors, we will need advanced Artificial Intelligence based sensors to provide efficient interactions between the tyres and the OBD modules."

"This is where Future Sensors come into the picture Mr. van Guard," Krish took over from Roshni. "The Future Sensors patent portfolio is all about AI-based sensors. They have a niche technology and very well planned patent portfolio."

"They must be very well funded to afford such a strong patent portfolio," said Mr. Chopra.

"Not necessary. We have talked about this before. Plus, if you know, there is also the Startup India programme by the government that provides free consultation and various benefits to startups to file patents."

"Now, Mr. Geert, you may know this, but let me explain this to the others. Patents are a negative right and that relatively less understood concept of patents plays an important role here."

Krish went on to explain the whole scarecrow example and the modification with wheels to clarify the concept of negative rights.

"So, while FS can never use your technology to manufacture tyres for vehicles since your technology requires their IP, they can sure stop you from the application of your technology in a vehicle. And therefore, however great your technology may be, you are now hopelessly reliant on FS and their patents to commercialize your technology. Unless you get a licence from FS or work a settlement with them, your project is a no starter. And FS seems to know this very well."

"Over to you, Roshni," paused Krish and went back to his seat.

Mr. Geert was the most experienced IP person in the meeting, having more than three decades of IP experience. But he had never before heard such a clear explanation to patents being negative rights as Krish had just explained.

"Mr. Geert, when I was interviewing our team members and yours, they came up with lots of possible applications and embodiments, which could have been better covered in the patents filed. Now, I understand that you have much more experience than me or anyone else in the room, but I wanted to ask you if you had a detailed discussion with the technology and business teams to plan a roadmap for IP filing in alignment with the technology and business strategies."

"Thanks, Roshni, for asking that question. I am not offended at all, rather, I am glad that we are discussing this, more so in the presence of some business and technology leaders. The short answer to your question is yes and no. The patent applications we drafted and filed were largely based on the invention disclosure and related content provided to us. As a part of our process, we did have meetings with the technology team to understand the details. However, for each application we filed, we met different inventors who explained the idea but could not provide us with the bigger picture. And there is always a pressure to draft and file at the earliest to claim an early priority date so we had to draft the patent application based on the information available."

Mr. Geert appeared calm and prepared for the question. He seemed as if he was looking for an opportunity to be heard on this topic. As ahead of an IP Department, it was a constant struggle for him to balance between the legal and business aspects of technology protection.

"We did not have a broader understanding of how the technology and business teams were thinking of this from a product perspective. In spite of multiple requests to be included in technology and product roadmap discussions, we were not invited. And this happens often. They see us as a road blocker and believe that if we join those meetings, we will always find reasons to delay things. The truth rather is that any project requires a proper IP due diligence to identify the risks and take corrective actions. This might, in some cases, cause some delay but is always beneficial in the long run. What is happening today is a perfect example of the consequences of what we try to avoid."

There was silence in the room for a few seconds before Roshni tried to continue the discussion.

"I hear you, Mr. Geert, and there is a lot that we need to do," continued Roshni "Another question I had for you was did you carry out technology and patent landscape analysis to understand the domain and the white space? I have read a lot about the importance and value of such an analysis when I was reading about patenting in general."

"You have used too many buzz words in a single sentence, Roshni, landscape, white space, domain analysis." Mr. Geert responded with a smile, with the tone of an expert responding to a novice who had just learnt some new keywords.

"You see, landscape analysis has become a fancy term in the last decade. A fancy term with a fancy deliverable having fancy charts. That is how I look at it. We have been doing it for long but in simpler ways. But if we remove the fancy keywords, the analysis is still important and worth it. And yes, we did a landscape analysis and shared the results with the business team. What I learnt was some of the charts from our analysis were selectively used in the business plan slides wherever they could strengthen the business case and the rest, ignored. And once again, we never got an opportunity to brainstorm the analysis results with the business and technology teams. In fact, we had highlighted sensors as an allied area to the technology based on patent classification analysis."

Krish was listening to the discussion patiently. This is not the first time he was hearing such comments from an IP team member. In his experience, this was a common malaise plaguing the technology industry. IP process was considered a roadblock by the business.

"You see, what is happening here is a total disregard for the basic IP planning," Krish took over, sounding slightly frustrated.

"I am sorry to say, Mr. van Guard, that you have an IP team, but you do not have an IP strategy. A team does not equate to a strategy. And without a strategy, there is no point having any IP. An IP team cannot work in a silo. They should have a seat on the strategy table where technology, business and product are having a discussion about the future roadmap of the organization.

It is such an irony that we have a game-changing technology built from scratch, advanced through collaboration but neither of the collaborators handled IP efficiently. One is an old-world manufacturing firm unaware of the modern challenges and benefits of IP and the other, though fully aware, did not have a smart IP strategy.

On the other hand, we have a new age, IP savvy, technology startup who knows its strength and how to play it. When I reviewed the FS patent portfolio, I could clearly see how smartly they have created a portfolio that covers their core technology and gives them an edge in asserting their IP. At the same time, the filing strategy also shows a well thought out plan to keep the cost low.

And this does not come only through awareness, it is also a result of applying the awareness. I am sure the founders at FS did not just ask their lawyers to file patents to showcase to investors. They would have sat down with them and plotted a detailed plan on why, where, what and how. Something every technology and business firm should do."

There were no answers or questions from anyone. Krish's face appeared on the screen for almost a minute as the video conferencing application had voice-activated switching, which makes it odd.

Mr. van Guard finally appeared on the screen as he started speaking. Mr. van Guard, who was listening all the time and was mostly at the receiving end of the discussion, did not have much to say but raised a logical point.

"Overall, FS seem to have a very strong portfolio and we are in a bad situation. But to the extent I understand, it seems like an enemy has been preparing for an attack for a long time and finally decided to launch when the time was right. An enemy who has been watching you for long, following you and planning for your doom."

"That's one way to console yourself. I would rather suggest we call in Mr. Rocky for an initial discussion and initiate the process for a possible out-of-court settlement. Let's hear his ask first," opined Krish

"I agree. That's the best way to start moving towards a solution to this problem. I will send a formal response to the notice asking for a meeting," said Mr. Gowda.

"Yes, let's do that. In the meanwhile, Krish and I will continue our analysis towards our response and next steps," said Roshni, agreeing with Mr. Gowda.

Chapter 11

The Strategy and the Landscape

It was a meeting over lunch. Food was served in the boardroom for all the participants, which included the regular four from RoadKing and Krish. On the video conference were Mr. van Guard and Mr. Geert.

"Thanks, everyone, for joining us," started Roshni.

"As discussed in the last meeting, Krish and I have done some more research and would like to present our recommendations to the group. This may take more than an hour. So strap your seat belts and hold your lunches."

"What options do we have? How do we get out of this mess? Why are we wasting our time? Why don't we just pay him a few hundred thousand dollars and get ahead with our project? My team has invested their everything into this project over the last few years and it would be a shame if we let it go because of a patent case," Swami was hysterical.

"I have invited Mr. Rocky for a discussion in the afternoon. I am hoping he will be here by the time we end this meeting so we can meet him directly after this," Gowda informed the group.

"We don't know what he wants. Going by history, he may have more sinister plans than just extorting money," Swami continued his rant.

Mr. van Guard and Mr. Geert were the only two who were unaware of the past between Roshni and Rocky. Roshni had shared the details with Krish.

"Yes, you were right, Mr. van Guard, when you questioned the intent of Future Sensors and a hint of personal enmity in the last meeting," Mr. Chopra took the opportunity to give them the context and went on to share the background story briefly.

Hearing the story, Mr. van Guard sensed a chance to square the blame. In the last meeting, he was at the receiving end of all the talk around the lack of an IP strategy.

"Now I understand. You should have told me this before."

"Mr. van Guard, it is easy to get into a blame game. Irrespective of my history with Rocky or what he wants, the fact remains that we have an ineffective IP strategy that has been woefully exposed and has led us to this situation," Roshni immediately interrupted without allowing Mr. van Guard to divert from the agenda. There was a sense of ownership in her voice.

Amongst all the challenges and business uncertainty caused by this situation, one big positive Mr. Chopra could appreciate was the leadership of Roshni that was positively exposed. She had led the situation from the front in a way Mr. Chopra had wanted to see for long. This had been a good learning experience for her.

"Coming back to the topic, Krish and I have developed a plan in consultation with Mr. Geert, focusing not only on the immediate challenge at hand but also at the long-term prospects of managing innovation and IP. We want to propose some steps for RoadKing, and I hope Forest would also take note and adopt corresponding changes," continued Roshni.

"There are two broad themes for our plan—Innovation and IP and the connect between them." Roshni connected her laptop with the presenter cable and flashed a PowerPoint presentation on the screen.

In line with the trend of minimalistic presentations, the slide consisted of just two words in a large font—1. Innovation and 2. IP with a double-edged circular arrow connecting the two highlighting a loop between the two.

"Mr. Swamy, I vividly remember your explanation of Project VC when you first explained it to me and how you referred to the "Can we" innovation principle. So the question now is..." Roshni paused and clicked for the next slide; another high-fonted quote covered the whole slide.

"*Can we* build an innovation culture in our organization?" flashed on the slide.

"One of the things that we are proud of is our innovation quality. Mr. Swamy and his team have done an amazing job. But maybe it's time to democratize our innovation plan. While the research group should continue their focus on developing new ideas, it would be great to expand the innovation mindset beyond the research team. We have so many employees working in our manufacturing unit on the machines, business development and client support executives regularly interacting with our clients, meeting our customers. I talk to some of them during my carpool, my ad-hoc lunch sessions or in team meetings. Many of them have amazing ideas. But these ideas have no path and hence die down. If we can create a platform for these ideas to prosper and grow, some of them may be the next Project VC. So, we should work towards creating an innovation culture beyond our research team. Mr. Swamy, hope you agree." Roshni cajoled Swamy using his own "can we" innovation principle.

"The second area of focus should be on the protection of these ideas through patents or other means. Dad, you did great in identifying the need for research and innovation and hired Mr. Swamy for the same. You also gave him a free hand in his efforts, which gave us the game-changing technology that we have today. What we need now is an IP strategy that aligns with our business strategy.

One of the things that we heard last time from Mr. Geert and Krish is that IP and innovation need to co-exist. Innovation in any organization aims at solving a business problem and, in turn, providing value to the organization. A proper IP strategy can significantly enhance the value.

We propose hiring a dedicated IP professional. The IP person can provide information and advice on what the focus areas for research should be and also analyze new ideas germinating from the research group. This will also help us plan a pipeline of research projects to focus on in future.

That's all from me. I will now let Krish share his detailed landscape analysis of the domain and some important recommendations. And Mr. Geert, it is not just fancy charts; there is important analysis and serious insights."

Roshni invited Krish to the front of the room.

"Thanks, Roshni. I will give the CXO-level view here and not go into the details," started Krish and clicked on the laptop to move to the next slide.

The next slide was very unlike the previous large-font text slides. It was just a big Banyan tree and multiple other small and medium trees of different kinds covering most of the slide.

"You all must be wondering what this jungle is all about. Mr. Geert, I agree with you when you say that landscape has become more about fancy charts than real analysis. But my way of representing is beyond fancy charts. I would like to take it to a different level of visualization. I have just this one slide. I want you all to imagine a landscape. Long green pastures of land. Some animals grazing leisurely. Trees of all kinds spread around. Let's call this landscape the EV storage landscape, and let us assume each tree represents a technology and patent portfolio," Krish softened his tone as he spoke, imitating a guru delivering a sermon.

It seemed to be working, at least on Swamy.

"I can also hear some birds chirping," Swamy spoke softly as he pulled up his legs, crossed them on the chair and closed his eyes to visualize the landscape.

Krish did not give a direct response as. first, birds were not a part of his visualization plan and, second, he did not want to disturb Swamy's trance.

"I want you to focus on the trees for now. These are technology trees. The roots of the tree represent the base technology, the stem represents the patent portfolio and the fruits represent the products built using the technology and protected by the patents," continued Krish moving back to a regular business tone.

"If you look at the RoadKing tree, the roots are definitely strong. No doubt about it. The fruits, which represent the final product that we are building also, seem to be growing well. However, the stem of the tree seems to be struggling. If you remember plant biology, the stem is the one, which delivers the nutrients from the soil through the roots to the fruits. So, if the stem is not strong, the product will suffer.

And this is where Future is trying to hit us. They are trying to hurt our stem. You can also look around at the variety of trees in the landscape. There are large Banyan type trees, creepers on the ground and everything in between. All these represent different types of technology and patent portfolios. Our objective now is to strengthen the stem of the RoadKing tree. How do we do that?"

"File more patents? Is that the answer you are looking for?" Gowda who was mostly silent spoke up.

"Correct. The first option for you is to strengthen the stem organically, which means file more patents to provide a stronger connect between the roots and the fruits. But that'll take time and you don't have time on your side.

There is another option and that's where this landscape analysis is of great value, with or without fancy charts. And that is to identify another tree that can help you strengthen your stem. A partner, which may already have a good portfolio of patents in the AI sensors space that you can collaborate with or even buy out.

Our analysis has identified at least two other potential partners that have a decent portfolio in this space. Their patents in combination with your current portfolio will give you a good edge in any fight against Future or any other player in the future. Ironic how Future as a noun and future as an adjective appear in the same sentence as a threat to you.

I have shared the detailed analysis with Roshni with some other useful insights that can help RoadKing take some strategic steps towards developing a stronger IP plan."

"So, how would a Future tree look like in your landscape?" questioned Mr. Geert, once again amazed by Krish's skill to communicate and present a complicated topic in a simple way using an easy-to-relate analogy.

"Glad you asked. The Future tree has strong roots as a result of its strong technology, and it sure has a very strong stem, as we have already seen. Interestingly, it does not have any fruits, as it does not build any products of its own. It provides support to other trees that can leverage Future's strong roots and stem to nurture their fruits or in other words, they are licensing their technology and patents to other players to build products. We may want to call it patents as a service! PAAS, anyone?"

"Future is ..." Krish was interrupted by a soft knock at the door.

Sumitha leaned in the door and announced that Mr. Rocky Dandekar was at the reception for a meeting.

"That's early. Probably, he is too excited by the prospects of an out-of-court settlement and the opportunity to make some money," Mr. Chopra scoffed. "Let him wait for 15 minutes."

"I won't suggest that. Let's get done with it," Roshni commanded. "Send him in. Or wait. I will come out to escort him in," and Roshni left the room with Sumitha.

Chapter 12
IP, the Great Leveler

Mr. Chopra had never met Rocky or even seen him or his picture. He had no clue how he looked. However, as we always have, he had an appearance in his mind. The build in his mind was tall, the face was a bit hazy and the overall appearance was rude and arrogant.

As Roshni returned to the boardroom with the most wanted figure in the room, Mr. Chopra's appearance of Rocky in his mind was shattered.

The person who accompanied Roshni in the room was short and spectacled with curly hair and a limp as he walked.

No words were exchanged as Roshni directed Rocky to take a chair towards the front of the table. There was a palpable stiffness in their body language.

There was an awkward silence in the room for a few seconds before Mr. Chopra initiated the conversation.

"Mr. Dandekar, I will come directly to the point. You are here for a negotiation. I have participated in many negotiations in my life. I believe in hard but honest and fair negotiation. I know my position today. You have an edge. You can call the shots. You can set the terms. So, I will let you quote an amount. What do you think is a fair value of your patents?"

"Would it be a few hundred thousand or will he go rogue and demand a few millions? Or is it more than money for him?" Swamy was calculating in his mind as everyone was waiting for a response from Rocky

"Good afternoon, everyone. I hope I don't need to introduce myself. I must say I am delighted to be here and in this position. It was a long-cherished dream for me. And Mr. Chopra, yes, I know my strength and I have always known it, be it as a student in college with Roshni or as a founder of a startup today. I love negotiating too, although I may not have as much experience as you have. But as you might know, I always believe that the less experienced and the less privileged can make up with passion and hard work and, must I say, strategy.

Mr. Chopra, if you know the history between Roshni and me, you would know that I am a strong supporter of providing a level ground to the lesser privileged. I have always championed that cause. The same applies to business. Just because you have a big organization and a strong legal team, you are not protected. If you do not innovate, you are at risk. And if you don't protect your innovation, you are at a bigger risk.

And in this sense, IP is a great leveler. It provides common ground to all innovators. It does not see who you are and what your background is. It only awards you for your creativity. What I am going to demand today is beyond money."

"Ohh, it is really more than money for him. This is a real revenge moment for him. To show his supremacy. We are doomed." Swamy's mind and heart, both were racing

"I understand, before I arrived, you all were discussing your IP strategy for future and Roshni and Krish presented a plan and some recommendations. I want you to enforce those religiously without fail. That is my ask."

"What does this mean? How is this revenge? And how does he know all this? Is there an insider plotting with him?" Swamy's thoughts were on overdrive as he glanced around the room.

There was immediate bewilderment in the room as everyone was trying to process what Rocky just said.

As Mr. Chopra was staring at Roshni, trying to make sense of what was going on, she stood up and walked towards the front of the room. As she was walking, Krish also joined her by the side and, finally, Rocky rose and stood on the other side of Roshni.

The rest in the room and on the video conference were watching the trio in amazement, waiting for them to unfold the mystery.

"Dad, you remember the day I returned from the US? In the car, on the way back home, you had asked me about my relationship status, and I had replied that when the time is right, you will be the first one to know."

"How is this relevant here? Please come to the point, Roshni," Swamy was struggling with the ambiguity

"The right time is now. And I want to share with you today that Rocky and I are in a relationship for over two years now. I know it sounds strange, knowing our background, but things happened. After the turbulent past we had in our engineering college, I was glad I may never see him again, but fate had other plans. Rocky was enrolled for a PhD in the same college in the US where I went for my MBA. We bumped into each other in campus and long story short, we bumped into each other more often and got to know each other better."

"Let me accept. I was struggling," Rocky took over. "A new country, a very different campus culture and the pressure of PhD were taking a toll on me. Roshni could relate to that from her previous campus experience and burying our past differences tried to help me. That is when I could see the love and passion behind the privileged front."

Cupid works overtime in campuses and in strange ways.

"My PhD research was focused on AI-based sensors. While pursuing my research, I got support from the university entrepreneurship cell to file a few patents. That's when I realized the power of IP and delved deeper into it. Around the same time, I incorporated a firm in India and worked towards commercializing the technology. I also got support from the Startup India programme on filing patents on the later modifications, and today, we have one of most advanced patent portfolios in the space. It helped us negotiate strong licensing deals with some big names, who did have a lot of money but did not have strong IP because they never planned for it"

"When I was interacting with Mr. Swamy and his team, I realized that we were doing something wrong about the way we were handling our research and technology. I just did not know what it was," Roshni continued.

"That is when I accidentally met Krish. He explained to me the whole concept of IP and I found the missing piece. I was also reminded that Rocky would refer to patents and IP for his startup though I never thought much about it then.

At RoadKing, we were seriously belittling our innovation effort without proper patent filing. And from what I heard from Mr. Swami and Mr. Gowda, it seemed none of you had any faith in patents. It would have been a no starter if I had just come to you and asked you to invest on a strong IP strategy.

That's when I hatched this whole plan. Rocky, Krish and I conspired to highlight the importance of

IP and get you all to believe in it. The only two ways to get someone to believe in something are—hope and fear. I thought fear would have a better effect on you and it seemed to have worked."

It was Krish's turn to unveil his part of the plot.

"It is true that FS is one of the best tech startups around and has a strong portfolio of very well-drafted patents. However, none of them relates to the Project VC and there is no threat whatsoever. Mr. Geert also hopped on our plan later when he read the Future patents and just could not see any threat because there was none.

Even the notice that was sent was not legit. I wrote a simple letter and sent to your office as a notice, which acted as a catalyst for you to get all the IP due diligence done. The landscape analysis that we have done is however very much valid, and I would strongly urge you to consider the recommendations. What happened was not real but is very much a possibility if you are not prepared. That's the message we wanted to send," closed Krish.

Though others were still grappling with the sudden turn of events in the room, Mr. Chopra was elated. In a rather unexpected way, his decision to let Roshni lead Project VC had proved to be another of his successful decisions.

"So, when I say that IP is a great leveler, I mean it. What education gave to me as an underprivileged child, IP gave me the same power as a bootstrapping startup founder." Rocky was philosophical.

There was a lot of depth in that sentence, which only a few organizations realize. IP is a great leveler.

Thank You, Reader

Dear Reader,

If you have come this far, then it means that you have read the book. Thanks for reading and congratulations on your interest in the topic of innovation and IP. I hope you liked the book and the idea of explaining a professional topic through a fictional story, for which I have coined a new term – Knowledge Fiction.

Innovation is a topic that is close to my heart and I am always looking for some constructive brainstorming on the topic to hear diverse views and experiences. I would be very happy to know your feedback on the book and any ideas to extend the genre of Knowledge Fiction writing.

I have also created two puzzles related to the book contents to rack your brains. Check them out in the following pages.

Do share your thoughts (and puzzle solutions☺) with me at sureauth@gmail.com or scan the below QR code, which links to a LinkedIn group where you can share your comments.

Puzzle 1 (Easy)

WordFind

Find 15 hidden words related to IP and Innovation from the book (Horizontal, Vertical, and Diagonal)

W	C	S	R	H	J	Z	Q	U	I	O	D	X	U	L	Y	B	N	M	E
I	N	F	R	I	N	G	E	M	E	N	T	H	H	A	G	T	W	D	F
D	E	C	E	S	J	K	X	R	T	Y	A	M	E	N	O	V	E	L	R
H	J	X	S	F	K	L	I	T	B	M	A	M	S	D	Y	H	N	S	H
D	C	E	E	F	B	S	N	A	O	X	E	T	V	S	I	U	F	C	R
V	A	U	A	R	T	C	N	V	B	Q	A	Z	X	C	E	R	N	A	M
Y	G	T	R	C	P	R	O	V	I	S	I	O	N	A	L	B	L	U	E
P	A	E	C	B	K	L	V	C	E	T	H	X	W	P	A	K	M	T	I
L	T	J	H	A	Z	X	A	S	D	F	G	L	I	E	R	N	K	O	S
S	E	W	P	O	P	A	T	E	N	T	R	B	I	O	N	T	I	M	S
D	R	V	G	E	W	G	I	K	M	R	W	U	R	C	Y	C	L	O	N
I	N	V	E	N	T	I	O	N	T	A	E	J	R	O	E	T	E	B	S
S	T	O	L	L	H	O	N	E	Y	D	R	M	B	P	D	N	T	I	N
R	Y	E	T	U	E	B	V	A	S	E	A	R	F	Y	C	I	S	L	E
U	U	F	H	I	N	R	S	X	C	M	S	G	V	R	I	C	K	E	T
P	B	O	N	O	D	E	S	B	N	A	D	N	U	I	U	K	I	G	H
T	H	E	E	U	S	K	L	S	T	R	A	T	E	G	Y	R	E	U	I
C	N	U	T	S	E	N	D	T	Y	K	C	E	O	H	W	B	V	B	D
D	A	R	T	A	K	E	R	E	T	P	V	F	M	T	O	N	E	R	Y
W	I	B	O	N	T	A	W	E	R	A	B	B	T	X	L	Y	O	N	S

Puzzle 2 (Difficult)

The Great Leveler Crossword

Some clues are straight, some are cryptic; some related to the book and some general knowledge

The Great Leveler Crossword

Across

1. A small hotel with a sustained applause by an audience is what patents protect (10)

6. The reliable source Roshni found while searching for "difference between patent and trademark" in Chapter 5 (4)

8. Car dial smashed to form a far-reaching group of atoms (7)

9. Eddie's offspring, a famous inventor (6)

12. No arctic melting is a generally prohibited drug (8)

15. Often used expression on social media found in a nemo jigsaw (5)

19. A 2015 comedy-drama starring Robert De Niro and Anne Hathaway (6)

21. A little over half improvement is required for an acting performance without preparation (6)

22. An indefinite and very long period of time (4)

23. A filed patent would reach this stage if it passes the examination process (5)

25. Eleven comes before twelve and _____ _____ (5,3)

28. A belief that helped me publish this book (6)

30. A micron, when mixed up, pioneered the invention of long distance radio transmission (7)

32. Zero cat have one life less than other cats (4)

33. The type of Intellectual Property that gives authors ownership to their books (10)

Down

1. What Future Sensors accused RoadKing of doing with its patents (10)

2. A logic gate which produces an output which is false only if all its inputs are true (4)

3. A frech velvet hook developed through accidental innovation (6)

4. A machine part that helps in reversing loot (4)

5. A book like this one, which is also new (5)

6. A famous NZ fruit mashed up to develop a collaborative website managed by a community of users (4)

7. A type of innovation that promotes collaboration beyond one's organization (4)

10. Everyone should have one as MLK Jr. had (5)

11. Do this to keep yourself high on Google search results (3)

13. You and ten together can create a melody (4)

14. Where it all started and soon we were all working from home (5)

16. More of these lead to more of 1 Across (10)

18. The clue for this is hidden somewhere between chin to nose (4)

20. A short input output after a mouse defines the required balance (5)

24. The hardest worker (3)

26. A sixth British nobleman, this one is pre filled (6)

27. A cine goofup led to the first programmable electronic digital computer (5)

28. A fascinating field of technology used in Project VC (4)

29. It is dime a dozen but can also change your life (4)

30. A single male, Yes, can produce a lot of .... (4)

31. Take a pledge to remove the start and end of loathe (4)

www.ingramcontent.com/pod-product-compliance
Lightning Source LLC
Chambersburg PA
CBHW030750180526
45163CB00003B/972